WAKE UP AMERICA AND GO TO WORK!

A LEADERS GUIDE TO FOLLOWING

I0469913

WAKE UP AMERICA AND GO TO WORK!

A LEADER'S GUIDE TO FOLLOWING

Written by Bob Smallwood

First edition

Edited by Sonjia Woode

Associate Editors;

Dr. Lory Britt, Laura Edwards, Star Gilmore, Dick Miller, Dave Post

Copyright 2013 Bob Smallwood

This book is dedicated to Thomas.
I pray that you find peace.

The following teachers, mentors and
bosses deserve special thanks:

"Plans fail for lack of counsel, but with many advisers
they succeed" Proverbs 15:22

Dr. Khonda Andrews, Barry Benedict, Don Boyce,
Steve Calhoun, Raina Childers, Bill Clark, Chuck Colby,
Ken DeLine, Dwight Ebling, Dwight Haley,
Kathy Hoffmeyer, Alan Horner, Bill Kipp,
Stewart Lauper, Dick Miller, Pete Merkel, Andy Nelson,
Doug Ohara, Bob Orlando, Peyton Quinn, John Rankin,
Bill Schaffer, Shelley Smith, Rollie Sumwalt,
Bill Sweeney, Elise Walton and Sonjia Woode.

Book Description

Having the unique perspective of a Christian, American manufacturing business leader and Chinese martial artist; Bob looks into the melding of our two cultures and what this means to our economy, our environment and our freedom of religion. Warning America that we are about to be conquered by the pen and the sword, Bob underscores our need to dig deep to resurrect the post WWII American work ethic and apply this to our efforts to turn the economy around. God doesn't expect us to stop working just because we don't have a job. In fact He expects us to step up the pace. What's happening in America is we are being conditioned to depend on government handouts instead of taking the risks needed to compete for entry level jobs. There are jobs out there and ladders to climb! More than ever before there are Americans doing nothing all day long. Equally as bad, our large companies are wrought with ineffective managers, wasteful, non-value added jobs in the middle and minimal paying jobs to our least qualified, hardest working Americans on the front lines. Combine this with an out of control litigious society and no wonder our corporations are moving to China.

Naturally the solution is spiritual. Maintaining a positive individual countenance is critical. This is best done through a mind steeped in thanks, and activities that focus on helping others. Begin each day asking God what He wants us to do for Him instead of asking Him what He can do for us! There is nothing more spiritual than doing His work first each day. Pray, sing, go to church all you want, but He expects work and obedience for His blessings.

Underscoring the important role that excellent individual countenance and performance plays in the turnaround of our economy, Bob challenges Americans to honestly examine their own capabilities and daily performance whether one is employed or not. As "Uncle Sam" asks; are you all that you can be?

Bob challenges the need for classic managerial roles including our need for "bosses". We only need "bosses" if we don't hire qualified, English speaking people who are responsible and hard working. Bob asserts that we don't have a leadership crisis in this country, we have a followership deficiency. Everybody wants to be the Chief, nobody wants to be an Indian anymore. (Oh Oh, is that not politically correct?) Bob addresses the role that coveting plays in this endless American drama.

We don't honor the kind of work that made America, "America" anymore. Our nation was built on the sweat and tears of farmers, steel mill workers, miners, assemblers, welders, teachers, secretaries, nurses, and tradesmen. There are Americans that believe many jobs are beneath them. Some of these jobs are being done in China by people working for American companies for slave wages in horrific conditions in factories that pollute our environment at will. We are more than able to compete and win in this global market place, but we need to demand a level international playing field with regards to the safety of their slaves and how their processes effect the environment. Pollution knows no national boundaries. Bob asks why we allow goods to be sold in America that are manufactured unsafely and pollute our air and water. Beijing is presently so polluted that respirators are required just to be outside!

Americans need to work smarter, harder and complain less. We are at war. We need to behave that way. We need to have a greater understanding of how important our role as followers is to God and our nation. Should we abandon patriotism for a larger world view? Not as long as we are One Nation under God, and China is not! It is our job as Christians to teach these people who have been denied access to His truth. There are 1 billion souls to save and bring to Christ! That's a lot of evangelizing. Wake up America! We have much work to do before Christ is ready to return. But be ready! Like any good boss, He wants to see us working when He gets here.

BIOGRAPHY

Bob Smallwood's 36 year career in manufacturing was spent working for some of our nation's most successful businesses in a variety of industries. He began his career pouring iron in the foundry at North American Rockwell's Draper Division in Hopedale, Massachusetts in 1972. He retired in 2008 from his position as President and CEO of SEMO Milling, LLC, a bio-fuel technology company and food grade corn mill in Cape Girardeau, Missouri. Prior to this he was a General Manager at one of our country's finest integrated packaging companies for over a decade. He was lauded for his ability to motivate work forces and won "Plant of the year" and "Employee Loyalty" honors more than once for a world class business with over 75 large divisions.

Today Bob is the Assistant Chief for a small Colorado mountain village volunteer fire department and owner/lead instructor of American Hero Response Training (http:/www.americanherort.com), a small business that trains firefighters, search & rescue personnel and civilians on crisis response skills, fire arm safety and martial arts. Bob is the Chief of Security at the Historic Crags Lodge, a Diamond Resorts International destination. He is also an active volunteer at the Crossroads Ministry, a non-denominational food bank in Estes Park, Colorado. In the summer he performs with his guitar and banjo for Rocky Mountain tourists. Most importantly, Bob is a happy Christian.

Bob is a graduate of Bowdoin College in Brunswick, Maine with a degree in economics. He has been passionate about the study of work, wisdom and the martial arts all of his life. "Warthog" as he was known, was a football standout and coach at Bowdoin. As a champion martial artist who competed at the state and national level, Bob knows what it takes to win as an individual or a team. More importantly, he knows what it takes to lose.

As a career manufacturing executive, Bob is intimate with the erosion of our American manufacturing base and the methods used in third world countries to "out compete" our own producers of goods that fill the aisles of Wal-Mart and Best Buy. As an industrial engineer, Bob has designed assembly systems and incentive programs for Fortune 500 manufacturers. As a Human Resource professional, he has been the key decision maker for over two decades with regards to hiring practices, performance measurement and progressive disciplinary actions. As an entrepreneur, he has successfully created and started up businesses from dreams, sweat and sacrifice.

Bob lives in Glen Haven, Colorado with his two cats and two horses. When not on one of his horses, he can be found on a Harley during the summer or one of his favorite slopes in the winter. Bob is a martial artist, singer, song writer and author who loves America, his mom and Jesus.

Table of Contents

INTRODUCTION
WAKE UP AMERICA AND GO TO WORK!
A LEADER'S GUIDE TO FOLLOWING

"The thoughts of the industrious always bring forth
abundance: but every sluggard is always in want."
Proverbs 21:5

Are you ready for your new Chinese boss, landlord or
Governor? I hope you understand that at this time most
people from China don't believe in the God of Jacob,
Isaac and Abraham. They have lived for decades with
no freedom of religion and a belief that everything
comes from the state. As a lifelong student of
Confucius, Lao Tzu, and Chuang Tzu; I can tell you that
you have nothing to fear unless expressing your faith in
Jesus is really important to you. But go ahead buy
products manufactured in third world countries. You
may as well give your money to some Chinese person so
he can afford to buy your property from your mortgage
company. They make great landlords; just put your
respirator on and take a tour of any Chinese village.

In mid February in 2012 I took a trip down memory lane
during a quest for obtaining hay to feed my two horses,
Dixie and Liberty. For over a decade I was the General
Manager of a successful manufacturing business in the
small Colorado town of Windsor. We were one of
Kodak's key suppliers in the production and distribution
of film. I started my career working in the film business

11

when digital was only a concept. At that time, I never thought that film would ever become obsolete. Our business was considered the best of the best in our industry, from profitability, quality, technological leadership and business culture standpoints. Kodak built the ultimate modern film factory in Windsor, Colorado in 1974. Today Kodak, one of the world's most popular brand names is bankrupt. The Kodak manufacturing facility is being dismantled, while the plant that I ran sits empty and idle.

One of the last major projects that I directed for Kodak was the design and manufacture of work stations for the manual production of corrugated boxes to package x-ray film for their operation in China. These work stations were for manual assembly, like it was done in the "old days", the 1930's! It was cheaper to pay two hundred Chinese workers than to pay 18 Americans who operated machinery to automatically manufacture these boxes in clean, safe work environments. We transferred the work to slaves. We sold the American Dream for the new Chinese Reality.

As a small child, a regular rant of my father's was Charles Wilson's misquoted; "What is good for General Motors, is good for the nation" so popular in the Eisenhower years. Today GM is the largest auto maker by volume in China. Dad was Right! GM just announced another 2 Billion dollars in investments in China over the next year to reach production levels of 2 million vehicles a year. Every penny is being invested in China. Thank you Mr. President for using our money to bailout GM so they could give jobs to the Chinese.

I drove through the very cosmopolitan town of Windsor, Colorado heading to Severance, a town noted for its "Rocky Mountain Oysters" (deep fried bull testicles) and goose hunting. Severance, like Windsor, is a converted ranch town into a western motif bedroom community for Denver and Fort Collins. I purchased my horse Liberty here 15 years ago. I arrived at the farm that held several hundred bales of poor quality hay that hadn't been covered. I opened a bale to smell the hay. "Why you smell hay?" asked the new rancher who didn't have the experience to know to cover the hay. He had just moved here from China and had purchased this very expensive ranch last year as an "investment". In a strange way he reminded me of Eddie Albert on "Green Acres." So I told him why I smelled and tasted the hay. I informed him that because the hay was of poor quality exacerbated by leaving it to the harsh Colorado elements, it was only fit for cows and worth about $6.50 a bale as opposed to the going rate of over $12 a bale! Due to the droughts that were suffered in Texas last year, hay is almost impossible to find in Northern Colorado. He learned a very valuable ranch lesson while I saw another beautiful piece of the American way of life purchased by an intelligent Chinese businessman who now has a lot to learn about running a farm. But he will.

Make no mistake, I am an avid fan of pre-communist Chinese culture, food, history, philosophy and I am a devout 34 year student of the martial arts, specifically

Chinese martial arts. I know that our people can learn a great deal about work ethic and respect for elders, authority and self from them. We Americans had better embrace them and understand they won't tolerate our laziness and lack of commitment to our superiors, employers and country. Wake up and smell the tea America.

I drove back through Windsor and, although I only left in 2005, the town had changed so very much in 7 years. Windsor, Colorado has grown in the last 20 years like the outskirts of Detroit, Buffalo and Cleveland did in the fifties and sixties when I was a child. I was a big man in this town 8 years ago as the General Manager of one of the town's largest employers. Today I was the grey bearded old guy in a pick-up shopping for hay, just passing through. Today, I am the "Fool on the Hill" that John Lennon wrote about. To see the world going 'round, I sit with the grey beards at the gate of my favorite restaurant "The NotchTop" in Estes Park, Colorado and discuss the world's issues. This is a book about many life lessons that we've learned the hard way in our quest for a piece of the American Pie. This is also a book about leadership and following. One cannot lead until one knows how to follow well. One cannot truly follow until one follows out of love. Those who consistently follow well, typically end up leading.

We Americans may or may not lack the leadership needed to turn the nation around. It is time for the followers of this nation to work so well that we don't need human leadership anymore. This was God's

14

original plan to begin with, it was man who begged God for a king; God gave us Saul. America gave us Barack Hussein Obama, Really?!

I see many books about leadership written by all sorts of experts. I looked and looked the other day and didn't find anything written specifically about followership. Personally I don't think that we have a leadership crisis in this country, our leaders are selling us to China. They know where they are going. Manufacturing our stuff in third world countries is the most effective way to guarantee the return on investment needed to attract and keep investors. To quote Frank Knight; "In the long run all producers are forced to use the most efficient methods or give place to others who do."

I think that we have a followership crisis. I don't think that most of the followers understand where our leaders are taking us. I think we have too many people who want to be leaders that aren't born with the goods. Our society encourages people to aspire to leadership roles. But the very nature of the concept of a leader includes many followers. Therefore the ratio of natural born leaders to natural born followers involves 1 over many. This is by Divine design. A person may have years of experience, they may have received promotions or college degrees, but have they ever exhibited any natural ability to inspire peers to follow their lead? Do your leaders possess emotional intelligence and charisma? Are the team of people they lead world class performers? Are they happy leaders and are their subordinates, happy people? In the long run of life, this is what has the greatest value, lasting happiness.

World class performing, respected people tend to experience more joy in work than people who do the bare minimum each day for a lazy boss. "Lasting" implies from young to old (or dead). "Happiness" is defined differently by each of us, but we know it when we feel it. The greatest blessing we can receive in this life is happy living. Technology, beauty, intelligence, favor come and go through one's life experience, but the trick is to remain productively happy regardless of the circumstances and contribute according to your abilities with your best efforts. Having a sound faith in God and good relations with your family and intimates puts the icing on the cake and many believe are essential for having a happy life. But the cake is who you are as an adult contributor in your limited time here on earth. Do you really need a boss to ensure that you go to work each day, on time and do your best job? If so, you really need to look at yourself. There is a huge two fold competitive problem in America which greatly threatens our national security; sloth and valueless jobs. The problem is much bigger than we fat Americans could possibly imagine and I have quantified this in American factories for decades. TRUST ME! Our new Chinese bosses will not tolerate us!

"What do you do?" This is a common question asked when we first meet somebody. But "why do you do it?" and "how do you do it?" are questions that are more important when learning to understand somebody. I challenge all of us to look at these two questions with regards to ourselves. Are you a natural born leader, or a follower? Both are good and depend on one another to survive.

Remember that old saying: "work like you don't need the money, dance like nobody's watching and love like you'll never get hurt." Our greatest defense against losing our American way of life is to live with the enthusiasm that the parents of our Baby Boomers had when they returned from WWII. Most of us exist because they returned home from battle and just wanted to go to work each day and come home to a loving family in peace. To our parents, working very hard for very little was so much better than war. We have so much more already than they had to start with. All that is lacking is a unified American Spirit.

But people do need the money so dancing like nobody's looking is a lot different than working like money isn't necessary. But existence continues whether we have a job or not. Work should also continue. Maintaining joy and continuing to work are the most effective weapons against Depression, both personal and economic depression. Some of us are happy, but most of us don't look that way. Most of us experience both pain and sorrow in similar doses. What really matters is how we experience this pain and sorrow and in what direction we grow afterward.

It is better to follow somebody who knows where they're going if it's where one wants to be. Rather than trying to cut a new path for myself all of the time, I have learned to save the cutting for God. He published His path many years ago and many brilliant, gifted men and women have written wonderful works inspired by God to help people find abundant joy, healing, hope, love and peace. We tarnish the beautiful gift of "who we are" when we don't accept His gift of grace, as He means for us to receive it. God loves and honors good, loyal followers. The pay may not always reflect how important your job is to God at the time that the tasks are actually being performed. But there is great, lasting reward in doing a job well; this must become more important as money becomes more elusive if we are to create and maintain joy as our economy shifts and slides. Doing the best job that you understand how to do for a higher purpose will have to be focused upon rather than pay levels, benefits or what position one holds. There are a lot of Americans working countless hours a week and earning nothing for it or going deeper into debt because of it and they need to keep on trucking for this country to turn around.

More importantly, there are American Service people in hostile foreign lands risking their lives for us, we are not supposed to rest until they are all safely home. We are at war, ACT like it! There is a nation of over 1 billion people that are willing to "eat bitter" to take your livelihood from you. Our corporate leaders are more than willing to sell them your jobs as long as they live on slave wages, have minimal safety standards and pollute the environment just like we did in the fifties. To beat them we will have to learn to "eat bitter" too. Many of you Americans have eaten bitter for quite some time now, thank you. It's time for you to find joy.

Sorrow, sadness, jealousy, anger are typically considered emotions felt as a bad experience. "Ku lian" or "Eating bitter" is a kung fu saying that means "hard, painful work over time to gain skill". Only the living, feel pain, so pain should be a celebration of life. Pain usually spurns change; it is hurt, but not necessarily injury. Through time you will grow. This doesn't require a healing as much as it requires a surrender of ego most of the time. Injury requires healing, hurt requires learning. Much pain we create ourselves when we listen to our ego instead of our intuition and sense of conscience. When our ego tells us that we are the creators and we indulge in those prideful thoughts, we disconnect from the God who created us and our opportunities. Our ego tells us we should lead; our God tells us we should follow. There is a difference between excessive pride and self respect. The consequence for excessive pride is always pain. The Universal system is designed that way to help us learn to change, mature and become all God created us for. The consequence for self respect is respect from others.

We all have to work, we all have bosses, customers, spouses, pastors, landlords and we all have a government to follow. All of these things can bring pain. Pain helps us grow, as Nietzsche said: "what does not kill me makes me stronger". We humans inflict pain on ourselves as much as our external universe does. The pain that I'm addressing is the anxiety we cause

19

ourselves because we don't honor our own followership appropriately. We find ourselves not liking the supervisor we have, or the company we work for, or our teacher or our coach, or our President. Boy we sure liked this boss while we were interviewing for the job. Once we've been working for a while, we tend to think that our boss isn't as smart as we are. Most of this is foolish pride as opposed to having a superior who is truly inept or evil as we may cast them in our own internal life drama. This mind chatter is negative and detracts from your potential and joy.

The real issues that we should devote our mind chatter to are; what kind of subordinate was I today, what kind of employee was I, what kind of student, what kind of athlete or artist? Did I serve my God, Family & Country to the best of my ability all day long? The greatest antidote for anger or the blues is to fill our mind chatter with thanks and our activities with helping others. A grateful heart is the parent of all other virtues. This is always our choice and God's will. It is your spiritual duty to serve your God, family, employer and country to your utmost. Your faith is demonstrated through these works.

We should avoid judging others as seriously as one should avoid killing or adultery. We judge others by how we perceive their actions, and we judge ourselves by what we believe are our intentions. Being a good follower means we examine our own actions and leave it to God to judge the intentions of others. The more we focus on examining our own behavior and correcting it, the freer we become. Joyce Meyer said "freedom is when you can say yes to God, no to yourself and still be happy". If we set our own standards of behavior to what we expect of others and perform to that, our economy would improve by double digits as a result of becoming truly more competitive. Most importantly if each of us performed to our own self proclaimed performance standards, this usually far exceeds the demands most employers make on its teams today. As a result people will require less supervision and there will be fewer bosses, making each of us freer. As the global economy balances itself to accommodate our loss of jobs to slave labor in third world countries, we have to find new meaning for the work that needs to be done to improve the present economy. "Accept, adapt and act" is a saying I learned from an old kung fu master that I have studied under. We Americans need to get up and work whether we have a job or not, especially if we are collecting money from our government. The American Dream was envisioned in the minds of our forefathers working on farms, in the coal mines, steel mills and auto assembly lines of yesteryear. There was a time when American men and women were honored to work in factories and mills. How we used to do it is still being done in Chinese factories and mills today by people honored to have a job and future. Hope has moved to China and she likes it there because she is appreciated and honored. Every time an American gives up on Hope, our nation suffers a great loss of momentum on many levels. Your hope is expressed in your work.

Besides love, hope is our most powerful weapon against Chinese domination.

Never since our creation as a nation has America needed to have such sound leader/follower relationships in place to compete globally to continue to feed American families and not sink back to an economy like our Great Depression was. Each of us plays a part that collectively impacts momentum of recovery and improvement beyond. Strangely, the part we play is spiritual when it comes to impacting our collective countenance. Our individual countenance needs to continually stay positive and happy versus negative. This is a choice regardless of circumstance. The magnitude of impact that collective countenance has on growth or failure is staggering. This is why I get upset with the Tea Party and Wall Street Sitters. We should focus on following our leader, not trying to dethrone him. Leave the political campaigning until election time. Until then, get up, shut up and go to work! The job you want is being done by someone who is willing to work harder for less than you. So work harder for less and you will be rewarded. The system is designed this way. The new American Dream needs to include a picture of happy American people with simpler lives and fewer things than what we have come to expect. If we are going to compete globally then we will have to sacrifice what we have as things balance themselves out because the people we are competing against are willing to live with extremely less than what we expect in the current picture of the American Dream. This still leaves us with quite a bit more stuff than the average person on our planet today, so be thankful and work.

We have the same President beginning a new term in a month. This is his last term, I never voted for him, I think he is a big problem, but I think that unity not strife is the answer. So "Tea Party" people give your excess money to the poor and to people needing money to start businesses, sit down, shut up and drink tea, get used to it. There is an old fighting saying; "the fight begins before the punch is thrown". China is training like Sly Stallone in the first "Rocky" movie and we are living like Charlie Sheen on "Two and Half Men" compared to them. Mr. President, get out of bed with China. AMERICA, STOP SELLING OUR SOULS AND CAPITAL TO CHINA and PREPARE. Iran and North Korea consider themselves at war with us already and the Israel situation with Gaza and Syria is a powder keg sitting near an open fire. Wall Street sitters get up, pick up a shovel and clean up the sand from Sandy, then get a job.

It is imperative that we have a mental environment in which we trust our leaders, our bosses, our company, our government and our schools to live happily and productively in these organizations. Even though it is hard to follow out of love when one has a boss that lacks integrity and work ethic. Leaders need to lead with integrity at all times. But followers need to work with integrity at all times and this means producing to the best of your ability at all times regardless of who your boss is. Never before in our history have we needed the followers in this country to get up and be the best followers on earth. Never mind your bosses integrity, worry about your own. Integrity is God's will being expressed by one of us humans through action and word. How do we know what God's will is? Look it up, Google it! God's will, in all things has been documented by so many authors. Pick an author with a several thousand year reputation for wisdom. I always say follow the dead first. After all, that's where we are going. The longer they've been dead the better; King David, King Solomon and Jesus had it goin' on! When somebody like Solomon who has been dead about 2,700 years, is still a best-selling author, read his books! When the boss is a jerk, follow old Sol! He won't lead you astray. But still remember, your boss is your boss. Understand that your superior was divinely selected for you to bring you pain to help you grow. I was asked once if following was about accepting pain and then somehow being spurred to grow and does this relieve the pain eventually? When you can see that the pain you are experiencing is temporary and yields results then yes, accept the pain. Pushups yield strength. If the pain leads to injury, try and understand the pain before you run from it. Maybe it's time to leave, if you cannot right now, yes accept the pain, work with integrity and God will provide other opportunities on His schedule, live patiently, this is God's Will. Be thankful. Remember your boss should help you, in fact make you grow. Growth usually hurts during some point in the process, cowboy up! If all your boss does is take attendance, parrot company spew and hand out paychecks, we really don't need him or her. We need you, boss-less!

Jesus said to Pilate, that he would have no authority over him at all unless God had given it to him. It is the same for your boss and our President. It is his or her time to be a boss and it is your turn to be their subordinate. It is OUR time to follow our President and conscience with all of our heart, body and soul. It is GOOD to "give to Caesar what is Caesar's". In this case being a good Godly follower is an enormous spiritual contribution to economic healing, government stability and security. Not since WWII has America needed such a national unity and effort. People the world over laugh at our nonsense. Most of our enemies are driven, skinny and convinced that they are morally right taking our nation down. They look at our division as a great weakness and our lack of respect for our leadership as morally wrong. Oh yes, most of our enemies; the North Koreans and Chinese, don't believe in the God of Jacob, Abraham, Isaac, Jesus and Muhammad. Our Islamic enemies simply and correctly believe that we are living our lives outside the guidelines of our collective Bibles. Just like ancient Rome and Greece, we are ripe for conquering. Old, fat, lazy, spoiled, "give me" Americans, we had better learn to speak Chinese, Arabic or Korean.

For purposes of discussion what is written in scripture is what I call God's will. You would be hard pressed to find a situation in our human condition that isn't addressed some way in our Bible. The answers written in the Bible are God's Will; anything contrary is not from the God of Abraham, Isaac and Jacob. However, I am an avid student of wisdom and history. Therefore I will quote anyone from the Dali Lama to Myomoto Mushashi. I know God has spoken to man since man set foot on this planet regardless of where on the earth and at what time God decided to express Himself. Many great masters have left mankind volumes of understanding. I enjoy indulging in all of it a little each day, and I always read a chapter out of the Bible before the sun goes down on every day. This is the most important part of my continuous improvement program for decades now. This naturally inspires thanks, peace, and hope.

As a general manager most of my career, I had people with PHDs and Master's Degrees in their chosen disciplines, working for me. They had a right to feel that I wasn't "Qualified" to be their boss! Often times I was brought into a business to turn it around. When I would arrive a team of very qualified people would reluctantly greet me as their new boss. Inevitably all of those people had wanted my new job. I walked in to jealousy, anger and resentment from people I hadn't even met yet. New bosses constantly deal with passive-aggressive nonsense from their new management teams. Most people have been programmed to covet the job above them, more than they've been conditioned to serve the person above them and do the job they have. This causes pain and inevitably slows progress to growth for them as individuals, but more importantly, to the organization and our national security. The rumor mill, the wait and see people, drain the whole organization as the new boss has to earn respect to gain trust, then true followership from his subordinates. At what point did it become more important to be a good leader than to always follow with enthusiasm and daily give one's best effort because it is the right thing to do? We wait for the leader to do his or her job before we hustle, if that is a word anymore. We allow people to constantly question authority, we allow lawsuits over nonsense, and we are more concerned with being politically correct or with peer pressure, than getting rid of the people that won't get with the program. We allow an entitlement mentality to exist because we are afraid to challenge people to improve their performance the longer they are with a company or God forbid, they are in a group protected by our EEOC. We want rules to enforce so we don't have to think and actually creatively lead. One leads people and manages systems. People always confuse management with leadership. People have a big problem with being judged, but leadership demands that a leader constantly judge and evaluate to keep his minions safe and on course. There are truly very few people able to judge fairly, so people in leadership positions should be few and far between, not based on some supervisor to worker ratio. Poor performers need to improve or starve. Stop feeding those who don't work. The only good sloth; is a dead sloth. Hungry people change behavior to find food.

Most of us have been programmed to want to lead. We're just not naturally capable. Where is the self-respect associated with working and doing your job well? Yes, flipping burgers is honorable if you do it well! Send all of us morons to leadership seminars all you want. We may improve our leadership skills, but I doubt it. I know it would be easier to teach followership and have it be effective. Most of us want respect, clear direction and expectation, then appropriate reward when we achieve those expectations. For most of us it's just easier to do the work, than to train somebody to do it. It is certainly easier to do the work than to truly motivate somebody to do it just like you or better. That's what leadership is; teaching, motivating and holding accountable, with an end to improve the performance of the team. Followership is doing what we're taught, how we're taught with an eye for spontaneous, proactive improvement but we are supposed to motivate ourselves. Any good leader is also a good follower. When you are a good follower, you follow well on your own. Be the subordinate that you would like to have!

Who needs this book? All people entering the workforce for the first time. Everybody who indulges in an inordinate amount of negative mind chatter or water cooler talk! Bosses need this, teachers need this, laborers need this, and geeks need this. People who are temporarily out of a job need this book. If your day includes a regular bitching session about your boss, company or country, then you need this. If you own a business or run an organization, you need to understand that if you want superior followership then your value system, mission statement and culture must mentally and financially reward great followers for following well. We Americans need to understand that our country is eroding to countries that are willing to work harder for less money in worse environments than we will. In this competitive world, quality and cost tend to determine where the work goes. Only superior organizations and individuals will succeed in the world market. Both organizations and individuals rely on constantly improving their performance to yield income to themselves and their stakeholders.

If you don't have a continuous improvement program for yourself that you adhere to, then you won't really improve. If you don't practice the piano, you won't play well. Nobody enjoys listening to poorly played instruments. Continuous improvement is a very personal paradigm to understand and incorporate into each individual's daily behaviors. In 2013 at the top of all continuous improvement lists for everybody should be to become a better follower. At the top of all organizational continuous improvement programs should be promoting a value system that honors working as a team towards continuous growth and improvement. Say no to the status quo! Each and every one of us can make a difference in turning our economy around and improving our national security by improving our daily contribution, our individual countenance and the quality of our work each and every day. Make a simple commitment for the New Year to cut your external complaining in half and double your internal thanks. Yes, this will contribute to better national productivity and security. Look at it this way, if we don't get off of our fat, lazy American derrieres' and get to work HARD now, our new Chinese boss will certainly make us when she gets here!

Chapter 1

Why do we work?

Four things are small on the earth, but they are exceedingly wise:

The ants are not a strong folk, but they prepare their food in the summer;

The Badgers are not a mighty folk, yet they make their houses in the rocks;

The locusts have no king, yet all of them go out in ranks;

The lizard you may grasp with the hands, yet it is in kings palaces. (Proverbs 30:24-28)

Obviously we work because most of us need the money to survive. Assuming that you are one of us, we go to work to give ourselves the best life possible. We work to get. We have a culture where the higher up the organizational chart you go, the more you get. We end up connecting getting more with moving up. I think that this works. We also work because it provides meaning. But where the disconnect comes into play are with the people who never move up, have no place to move up to, don't want to move up, or have no interest in moving anywhere but out the door as soon as the workday is done. What about these people? Unfortunately most of us think about what our jobs are going to provide us: benefits, pay, and hours? We really should be thinking about what God given talents do I have and how can I express them to the best of my ability, day after day. If what you do to make a living doesn't align with your

God given gifts and dreams then plan to find a living where that can happen. Until that happens, you cannot easily find happiness at work. It is certainly possible, but it is more difficult and it is also your responsibility, not the organization you serve or our government. It is difficult to follow if you are not happy on the way. Follow your path and your chosen leader to the best of your ability all of the time, that is all you can do. But in the long run this is so important to your happiness and our national security.

In the proverb that I started this chapter with, Solomon depicts what is exceedingly wise. Ants have the foresight to store provisions; badgers find protective shelter; locust have an ordered community; and the lizard is courageous. I want to focus on the locust first. Originally God didn't want us to have a king in our life. It wasn't His plan in 1 Samuel 8, He made that clear. From the beginning He wanted us to serve based on our conscience, our Holy Spirit that dwells within. It took Jesus of Nazareth to drive home the point that each of us has an internal divine-voice. Mankind didn't get it in Samuel's days. They demanded a king. God gave them Saul, selected for the job because he was a strikingly handsome and tall man. Get over it you ugly, short folk. It is the same today; all studies indicate that favor still goes to those who are good looking! God picked a nut. Saul was subject to panic attacks and became obsessed because David was considered a greater hero for killing more people than Saul had. Negligent hiring we would call it today; "discrimination!" would cry the ugly. Saul resigned in the harshest of ways, this is where the phrase "falling on his sword", comes from. Then God promoted David. David had a subordinate, Uriah, killed to cover the fact that David was shtoinking Uriah's wife. But God didn't fire David as king. It sure hurt his image though, just like it hurt Tiger Woods's and Bill Clinton's image. But what really pissed God off at David was when David took a census to calculate his chances for victory in battle. This from a guy who killed a giant with a sling shot because God said he should, now, years later, David tries to figure stuff out instead of trusting God's direction. The Divine rewards those who follow, not figure! He always has, He punished mankind for the eating of an apple, He punished Moses for striking a rock when Moses was told to speak to it, and therefore He'll punish us for falling short of His expectations. In this proverb, Solomon says that it is exceedingly wise to know your rank and conduct yourself accordingly without a boss, like the locusts. Be exceedingly wise every day.

In keeping with my philosophy of follow the dead first, I will use as examples, real heroes in my life who have passed away. I want to share their essence with you because it is the qualities of character that they expressed in their lives that our American people need to continue to embody. I will describe two great locusts who although they were the same critter, they expressed their locustness differently. God has provided a world for us to be a locust in and still be an individual. Hal Mason was "a great father, a loving Papaw. He was known by others as a wonderful brother, co-worker, best friend and neighbor. Halquin loved spending time with his grandson, watching kung-fu movies, taking care of his yard, collecting his eagles, waxing his car, working and playing the drums." Hal was an all American man. Hal was a great follower of his God and his leaders. I had just become the GM of the very large business that Hal worked for. True to my form, I arrived for my first day of work a day early so I could see the truth, not the show that was being prepared for me. I got there at quitting time to see which managers left early or at the bell and which managers stayed to get the job done. I was wearing a sleeveless Harley Davidson shirt, jeans and my old cowboy hat. I made one of the managers take me around the plant and introduce me to everybody on the second shift, over 150 people. Nobody expected the new GM to be dressed in jeans, nobody expected me until 8:00 am the next day. When I saw Hal I walked over to him and introduced myself, he didn't know that I was the new GM. I asked him how he was and he replied; "blessed beyond all measure!" He had such warmth to him, such strength and joy for life; he shined. I laughed as Hal was told that I was the new GM, it didn't faze him at all, and he smiled and welcomed me. We talked every day from that point on. Hal answered to God, this was obvious, Hal was happy! Hal was gregarious and fun. Hal sought to be respected for how hard he worked and how talented he was, Hal didn't need to be anybody's boss to feel good about himself and his life. Hal hustled! Hal died in an automobile collision. At his funeral I spoke on behalf of our company. The pastor gave a great eulogy. The theme of the pastor's talk was "Old School". Hal was "old school". He had the work ethic we all need. He knew that actions + behavior= consequences and he took responsibility for both. He didn't need to be asked to work 12 hour days when his coworker suffered with cancer. It could be 105 degrees in that plant day after day and Hal's smile was as bright as the Texas sun. Hal was never afraid to tell me if he thought something was wrong, he had courage, like the lizard. With a team of people like Hal, one doesn't need bosses! It wasn't Hal's position as much as his demonstration day in and day out of his devoted followership that made Hal a great American leader.

I took a friend on a trail ride yesterday. I informed her that I was writing this book and what it was about. I told her that I wanted the cover to be of a line of riders on this certain mountain ridge where the vista is spectacular and one would see the line of horses following me. I told her where I wanted the picture taken from and she said that from that angle one would not be able to see me on the lead horse. I said, "Exactly the point!" If the team is made up of good followers, the leader shouldn't be that visible. We weren't able to make that picture work, so we opted for me leading a single horse with no rider.

Locusts don't need a lead locust. Can you tell which locust is leading the swarm? They all do the right thing at the right time, simultaneously! The locust is actually a rather tasty thing if prepared right. It crackles beneath your feet. As a single creature it really has no power. But as a team, their power is devastating! Just like us humans.

Bonnie Shaw is another locust who God took early from us. Bonnie was my Information Systems Manager and worked for me at two different companies. She was one I took with me, because of her locustness. The most important part of being a locust is, genuinely possessing a truly shared purpose with everybody on the team. Bonnie was a frail woman who suffered with cancer for several years. Her courage was amazing as she came to work day after day. Bonnie and Hal were almost opposites in terms of personality, but they were both locusts. Bonnie was quiet and gracious. She served the whole team in her role. She was diligent, forthright, creative, and dependable. I am fairly inept when it comes to computers. Bonnie filled those gaps for me without ever feeling that she should be in a higher position because she knew more than I. She knew how I thought so she usually anticipated my needs and did this for everybody. Bonnie served us joyfully everyday up until she passed away at 42. Bonnie and Hal were great workers and great employees. They both made the workplace a happier place to be, they both gave a noble effort day in and day out. Having people like them as part of my life's story make me blessed beyond all measure. They demonstrated the qualities that we need from the people in our world every day. We should all strive to be content, if not happy in our current roles. We demonstrate that we aspire to move up with our performance of our current tasks in addition to what we are willing to do that make the team and our nation secure, productive and successful that are beyond our job descriptions.

We don't have a leadership crisis in this country, we have a followership crisis. I was as guilty as the next guy at times. I enjoyed a good boss bashing with peers as much as the next fellow. I sent personal emails on company time. I called in sick when I went skiing instead, and I listened to and shared gossip. I got caught up in company politics and gossiped about corporate decisions with the best of them. It was all wrong and I am ashamed of the times that I wasn't a good locust. That won't happen again. It won't happen because I truly see it as a cancer in our world that is killing our joy and security. It won't happen again because our new Chinese leaders won't allow that! If we educated our young that gossip and water cooler time was as bad as bullying or riding your bike without your helmet on, then we would start on the right track. Don't down talk your company or superior in front of your kids anymore than you would use a racial slur in front of them. I have been a martial artist for 34 years. In this capacity I have studied Asian cultures extensively. In my business I have competed with the Japanese and later the Chinese. Lao Tzu writes in Tao Te Ching, "the man of skill is a master to be looked up to by him who is unskilled; and he who is unskilled is the helper of, he who has the skills. If the one did not honor his master and the other did not rejoice in his helper, an observer, though intelligent, might greatly error about them." This means to the observer it may appear that one is over the other. But in reality one completes the other. They need each other to truly be themselves. One of the greatest assets that most Asian cultures share is their internal passion for excellence in doing their work as they seek excellence in everything they do. I had machines that produced 10,000 boxes an hour and produced 2% scrap on a good day. The same boxes were being made by hand in China, perfectly. Their cost was less, even though they had thousands of people folding boxes. These people were thankful that they had a job and they felt it an obligation to do the job perfectly in quantity and quality, all of the time. This is, to them, a prerequisite for considering oneself a good person. In ancient Japan the Samurai was dedicated to service. The very word samurai means "to serve", even if it means your life. Again, showing (having), respect for everybody and working hard are considered qualities that make one a good adult. Asians aren't late for work anymore than they would take a crap on the kitchen table. It just doesn't happen.

I love America! I love manufacturing. It is sad that so much of it is done in third world countries with slave labor and we just buy the stuff. Simon and Garfunkel wrote; "Where have you gone Joe DiMaggio?" They knew where he was when the song was written. But they weren't just talking about old Joe. They were crying out for the whereabouts of the American hero. I think that Tiger Woods was as close as we could get to the all American super hero, then his humanness got in the way just like King David's. How much time has been wasted on this? Nonsense, water cooler talk!

I received my Industrial Engineering education at General Motors Institute, now Kettering University in the late 70's. I learned to be a time study expert and a methods engineer. To the chagrin of those who are close to me, I time everything! I do work sample studies and time motion studies constantly on everything. Do you want to know how long it takes for the All American breakfast at the NotchTop Bakery to be served? I know that! Or how long it takes to get from the parking center at the airport to the gate, day by day? I know that.

When I ran manufacturing plants, especially assembly plants, knowing standard unit time was akin to knowing what time it is. I did work sample and time studies on all of my people, regularly. This means that I documented what each manager was doing 4 random times a day for 19 working days at a time. I accomplished this by making a checklist that included things like; talking on the phone, eating, walking, in meeting, on computer, directing subordinates, doing company reports, cell phone, gabbing, doing direct labor, doing indirect labor and in bathroom/cafeteria. I checked off what each person was doing as I passed them. After 20 days I made Pie Charts depicting statistically how each person spends their day. Here are some facts compiled scientifically over 30 years of study in a variety of industries and agencies; a GOOD salaried manager works 65% of the time. A GOOD direct labor person works over 88% of the time, this may include indirect labor, GOOD indirect laborers works 75% of the time. Higher level managers work 90% or better. Successful entrepreneurs and small business owners always work. These aren't average workers, these are the GOOD ones! Imagine how much our average manager works. I'm not talking about "do you go to work?" I'm talking about "do you actually do productive work while you are present?" Our average corporate manager is a little more than useless in most American companies. Ask the workers on the frontlines and factory floors, they know this is true. I can absolutely prove this! There is a huge chunk of Middle America that is disappearing. Our large corporations are bloated with people who get paid too much and don't produce anything of value. The rest of middle-America is working too hard for too little money. These are the laws of supply & demand and survival of the fittest (best) in action. This is a good thing in the long run if we don't get conquered while we figure it out.

Direct labor people actually move the rock, they change something. Judith Bardwick used an analogy about moving the rock that I have used in my career for 16 years. Suppose a landslide leaves a large rock on a roadway. We need to move this rock off to the side of the road. One person tries to move the rock, but cannot. Two more people try to help move the rock but together all three can't move it either. After three more people are added, they are able to move the rock. It took six people to move the rock, they all directly pushed the rock and they changed its location. Imagine that another person was added to the team to supervise the work, but he did not push the rock. Add another person to watch out for safety and add yet another to engineer the best way to push it. These added people indirectly help, but they don't move the rock. They are indirect labor. In this country we usually hire low skilled people who don't speak English. Then we ask some poor shmuck to watch over them. We think we are smart to pay these people as little as possible but we get as little as passable from these people, along with high absenteeism, poor quality, employee unrest, and process inflexibility. I have proven that we don't need classic supervision and we don't need to spend the money on indirect labor. Hire better people who don't need to be supervised and pay them! Hire good followers and very few able leaders.

I always do work sample studies during my first 30 days at any plant that I took over. Then I would deliver the good news to those whose efforts were exemplary and the bad news to those who spent their day screwing the pooch. Playtime's over boy! I don't give a crap who you play golf with or who you drink with. America, our managers don't work over 35% of the time that they are paid! Because they are not held accountable for their time like assembly line workers are, and they don't know what to do! They have this "with rank comes privilege" crap. They find tasks to hold on to and keep their bosses informed and out of trouble, but their contribution is questionable. Always treat everybody the same, from the company president to the janitor. The king and the pawn go back in the same box when the game is done. What always shocked the businesses that I took over was how directly I treated the managers, versus how politically I treated them. It also shocked those units with how much time I spent on a hot factory floor versus an air-conditioned board room. These are the people who move the rock, America! I can walk into any factory in the world for a day and tell you how it operates from an efficiency and safety standpoint. I have actually been blessed to lead two separate workforces to reach over a million man hours without a lost time injury in industries that are hazardous. It can be done. Factories that have no accidents are usually profitable. I guarantee you that in factories that have poor safety records, they have managers who actually work less than 40% of the time and they have no or poor profitability! I actually worked for several companies that gave kudos for time spent when managers played golf with their subordinates. But when it comes to laying people off, we cut the people who work 88% of the time, while the lazy people who work 40% keep their jobs and now have to work 43% of the time. Then they go home and complain to their wives about how hard they work. It is these employees that we fill the leadership seminars with! How about re-educating them on how to follow and do a day's work for a change. These are the locusts that need to be crushed beneath our feet; get up and fly and you won't get stepped on!

This isn't a new problem. There is a wonderful book called Perek Shirah an ancient Jewish text. Most credit David with its works and others credit Solomon. The words mean 'the Songs of the Universe'. There are 85 songs of creation, all of these are included in the song of heaven, "Truly, it declares the glory of God, its Creator!"

"From the towering Mount Everest and the mighty Amazon River to the industrious ant and the web-spinning spider, every part of creation sings it's praise to God and its message to man."

"When do they sing it? Every second. What is their song? Verses: that express the God-ordained tasks that they perform continuously. Every creature serves God perfectly and without interruption, for it does what it was created to do; it cannot do otherwise. These are the songs in Perek Shirah. Only man is the exception. He has no song in Perek Shirah. Why not?

Maharal the Talmudic scholar explains why. There is a basic difference between potential and performance. Potential is important, but only if it is realized; unrealized potential is worse than meaningless, it is a tragic waste. The songs of the creatures of this book (Perek Shirah) are not potential, not intermittent outbursts of ecstasy: they are constant, uninterrupted expressions of the instinctive mission which God instilled within them.

What Adam and Eve did to man when they ate that apple has kept us from having a song. It keeps us from doing the job that God ordained each of us to do, with the individual gifts with which God created us to express. It is that ego thing; lust of the eyes, lust of the flesh and pride of life. It is a sin we all need to work on keeping out of our lives, like racism. It is also a sin that costs us in America more each day than this recession has. Each one of us is capable of more, better, safer, smarter, faster, cleaner. The universe throws so many monkey wrenches into our works each day. We need to stop

42

throwing them into our own works by indulging in wasteful thoughts, words and actions that hurt our countenance and potential. Gossip, water-cooler talk, doing personal things on company time, doing nothing on company time, these are all sins. There is more untapped potential wealth in this country to be found by reducing this waste, than all of the oil in the Gulf could give us. This requires one of two things; having a boss that brings us pain to help us grow and do better, or be like a locust and do it ourselves; know our rank and fly!

We have a task at a horse ranch I used to work on as a wrangler that we call the "jingle". Twice a day we need to move 70 horses from one pasture area to another, but we have to herd them through a small residential section of the ranch. This requires precision and cooperation of the ranch residents. We announce that we are going to jingle and then people stop what they are doing, they move their trucks onto the roads to block the horses from straying down residential streets while we round up the horses then we move them through. A horse is a horse of course; they panic easily and their emotions are highly contagious within the herd. A horse is also a highly social animal; the pecking order is very important to them and is regularly challenged as part of normal herd behavior. All it takes is one leader horse to get a bug up his butt; this can wreak havoc on the behavior of the whole herd quickly. The lead wrangler needs to keep this behavior in check while on a horse that is trying to follow human direction, but is also greatly affected by herd behavior. It is easier to herd cows than horses for this reason. This is very similar to having a subordinate in a leadership position. You need to have a strong individual leader, who responds to your direction and cues. Don't forget, that these leaders are also affected by peer behavior, like a herd of horses. Put the alpha horses in the leadership role and the followers will follow. No matter how well you train a follower horse, he gets his butt kicked when he gets back in the herd after the ride is done and the herd pecking order resumes. This is like promoting the best worker, who isn't the actual leader of the group, to be the supervisor. He stops being the best worker and the group dynamic usually deteriorates. Let leaders lead and train them to do that well; let followers follow and honor them for doing that well. Then pay them both fairly. Both demand integrity to succeed, the head people have to be passionate about work environment, profit, integrity, personnel and environmental safety.

These are my Standard Bob Smallwood Company Rules; five don'ts, four do's. Don't be; dishonest, disrespectful, lazy, stupid or irresponsible. Do be; happy people, safely making, good stuff, fast. If we were making boxes, then it would be good boxes fast, if it was making microwave ovens it would be good microwave ovens fast. These are the only rules that I used while successfully operating large union-free factories for over 2 decades. Too many rules indicate a manager's attempt to systematize integrity in leadership, so the fewer the number of rules, the better it is. Work with principles, lead with integrity, be present and accessible, teach about safety and profitability and how each job impacts both and you won't need no "stinkin rules" man. As long as your product and service remain in demand, you will do well, it is Karma. If your reward system encourages people to be creative and do their best as a leader or follower, you will do better. When you find a bad horse in the herd, get rid of it. Yes, there are horses that are never safe, or are mean or simply pester the other horses in the herd. For everybody's safety and improved herd performance, get rid of it. This is one of the most important jobs of a leader; judgment and punishment. Most of us humans aren't capable of either so our companies shouldn't have layers of well meaning people trying.

The ant is industrious and stores food for the winter. WTF America! Can you do math? We blame politicians and Wall Street for our woes. How about plain stupid? We buy a house with a variable market value. We take out a mortgage, in some cases, a ballooning mortgage, at a fixed or increasing cost of 50% or more of our disposable income. Then we compare this to an income level that grows an average of 3% a year, if we get to keep our job. While you wrap your precious kid's head in a helmet to ride his bike, try putting some math skills and common sense into his head; maybe he will learn to do percentages, add and subtract. How could we not fail at some point in the cycle, especially when it takes two incomes to cover one mortgage? Not everybody deserves to own a home! This book isn't about personal finances. But, I will say unequivocally, when you don't have any debt and you have money in the bank, an enormous amount of mind chatter disappears! Life is better and pain is reduced!

The beauty of this is that most of us are capable of having this life after some sacrifice and hard work for a couple of decades. This can be done while tithing 10% of our income! I live very simply, a 1,200 sq. ft. cabin on 5 acres. I heat with my own wood, drink my own water; I do not kill my animal friends for food yet. Tithe, save money, live simply and work hard.......do not go into debt! In your young lifetime you can free your mind of debt pain. A 15 year old car that is paid for, rides better than a one year old car with a large monthly payment, when one loses one's job! Stop trying to keep up with the Jones! NEVER buy a car on credit! If you can't pay cash, use a bike like your Chinese brother does.

Let's talk about industrious! The ant is an amazing creature; like the locust, they are devastating as a team. One only needs to live in Texas for a while to experience the fire ant! The Perek Shirah says; "The ant is a living lesson in industry and dedication to general welfare. Each ant scurries in search of food and carries six times its own weight back to the communal nest. It lives for only six months, but gathers enough food to last it many lifetimes, as if demonstrating faith that God will give it longer life." There is always more to do, more to accomplish and more people to be served and helped. It is possible to be out of a job, but never run out of work.

Again Solomon's proverb says that it is exceedingly wise to be like the ant! Have you ever watched Texas fire ants? They work or attack as a team, immediately and totally! They embody spontaneous, orderly,

46

creative, instinctive activity towards an end. I have watched their symphony many times from my back porch in Texas. Here is a fact for you. From the time that it takes for a large grasshopper to get caught in a Black Widow's web, until the fire ants have taken the last remnants of it down into the earth, is 27 minutes 23 seconds! While the spider sucked the life out of this critter, the ants had begun to assemble in order to dismantle the carcass and carry it away. As soon as the spider left, the work began one ant at a time. I did not observe any ants taking smoking breaks, chatting off to the side, texting friends, sleeping under leaves, or giving directions to other ants. I saw no union organizing ants waiting off to the side to steal the working ant's pieces of grasshopper. I would love to lead workers like that, but I wouldn't have to lead. I would need to do two things; teach and guide them to the next meal. But God does that for the ants and he does that for us too!

The badger builds its home in the ground for safety and security. This is why we work! To live, thrive, and provide for our loved ones. We work to exchange our services for food, shelter and security. The ant and the locust tell us that we are naturally programmed to be industrious, and work for the good of our general welfare. The badger is about defending home ferociously, and selecting home strategically, for the good of the family. Again, Solomon says that this is exceedingly wise.

Understanding that those who are in the highest places in organizations get the most money, as a good badger, we want to make sure our young are taught values that motivate them to be 90% performers like those in top management. I'm not saying that these 90% people always do good work, or never make mistakes, but their work ethic shows day in and day out. This, combined with a little political savvy, eventually afford many an opportunity to sit as a senior manager. On the flip side, the consequences of being a 60% producer, or worse, should also be understood as a choice, and your responsibility to change this. As a badger, we want to have a secure home for ourselves. When our job performance is poor, we jeopardize the security of our home. We are not a good badger when we are on Match.com or EBay at work, when we sit in office after office and gossip, when we attend worthless meeting after worthless meeting and don't contribute, we are failing as badgers.

Badgers do not hang out with other badgers like prairie dogs who build a village of holes. They do not swarm and work as a team like the ant and locust. According to Bobby Lake-Thom in his book "Spirits of the Earth", the "badger is a good sign, meaning protection. But he can also warn of danger if you are traveling in a vehicle or walking. Badger medicine can be warrior medicine, doctor power, and protective power. He is courageous, tenacious and defensive." These are qualities that Solomon says make this nasty little critter exceedingly wise. These are also qualities of being a good parent and provider. This is why we work. The old American saying, "to build a better life for my children", that is why we work.

I knew a great badger, his name was Ken Colasuonno, and he died March 18, 2010. Ken and I taught Kenpo Karate together. Ken was an engineer for Hewlett Packard then Agilent Technologies. Ken was self claimed "enginerd". He was a great engineer and teacher. Ken had leadership qualities, but the quality that I admired about Ken more than his kindness and attention to detail, was his love for his family. Ken was a happy and extremely courageous man. Ken was a Boy Scout leader, he was on the Parent Advisory Board for an elementary school, and he went on mission trips to Mexico and built homes with Habitat for Humanity. Ken loved his kids. The greatest tribute to a father and husband I ever heard was given at his memorial service by his wife Sharon and his son Paul. Their poise and composer, combined with their awesome presentations were a tribute every father and husband would love to listen to from heaven. They couldn't have pulled it off, had they not known for sure that Ken was with the Lord. To know Ken, was to see God's will in action. The results for his living this way gave Ken a happy and abundant life. He had the respect of everybody who knew him. Actions + Behaviors = Consequences, always!

Security means more than a home in the rocks. If those rocks happen to be in a prairie that is soon to be damned up to build a lake, it won't help to have a home in the rocks. The badger will drown or have to move if he can. A smart badger would get the hell out of there when he first saw the land moving equipment. The dead, wet badger waited until the water came, like the people of

Noah's time. I spent a good part of my career servicing Kodak's film business. Teams that I have directed were six-sigma quality providers to the best businesses in the world: Motorola, HP, Lexmark, and yes, Kodak. I don't just talk six-sigma, I lived six-sigma. (For you non manufacturing folks, six-sigma means that your business produces only 3.4 defective parts per million parts produced.) But being supplier of the year couldn't save the film business once digital took hold. We were safe in the rocks, but the damn was built. Kodak's corporate organization did everything right as a team of manufacturers. But the thousands of people and the tens of square miles of manufacturing space that used to be devoted to film production, sit idle or are gone. So, in today's business world, being a good badger means constantly looking at our total work environment and the world market environment, in order to access our own skill sets and our company's technological survivability. I don't have sympathy for people who get laid off after 30 years of doing the same thing. What lasts thirty years? Get with the Bleeping program or drown when they fill the lake. It is our job as badgers to keep ourselves educated and our skill sets pertinent to today's changing market place. It is also our job to look to move as soon as the earth moving equipment starts digging, not when they start to fill the lake. Look to the future and understand the past. Keep these losers off the news.

The lizard being found in palaces is important, because the lizard is a lizard whether he is in a swamp or on a palace wall. He is unaware of the palace as significant. The Bible indicates that the lizard is credited with being courageous. Courage is not the absence of fear; courage is doing the right thing in the presence of fear. Solomon says that it is exceedingly wise to be courageous. What does courage have to do with the workplace in America? The reason that Solomon says that it is exceedingly wise to have courage has to do with the results of being courageous. The results of demonstrated courage are respect, trust, self-respect, love. All of these bring positive results. It takes courage to do the right thing when peer pressure pushes you in the opposite direction. It takes courage to tell your boss that he or she is wrong. It takes courage to say that you made a mistake. It takes courage to accept a promotion to a position that you know very little about. It takes courage to conduct a meeting. It takes courage to give a presentation. It takes courage to go visit a customer who was just very displeased with your company's product quality. It takes courage to facilitate the implementation of a policy that is unpopular, or to enforce a company rule or to tell a gossip to shut his or her mouth. Courage is recognized and usually rewarded when it comes time for raises and promotions. Yes, sometimes it can cost you your job. If your stance had integrity and your methods of communicating showed respect, and you still get fired, then you should work someplace else anyway. In many cases it takes courage to get up and go to work day after day with no hope of raises or promotions. If you are asked to do something unethical by your boss you shouldn't do it regardless of how much income you stand to lose, this takes courage. The single parent who shuttles from daycare to doctor's office, to work, to home, to cook, clean and care for kids, has a lot of courage to do this every day, especially when ends barely meet. There is a need for courage everyday for everybody. There was never a person who had more courage than Bonnie Shaw. She battled cancer for years, but did her job every day.

Although the lizard doesn't recognize the palace as significant, this doesn't mean that the lizard holds the palace in contempt. This isn't insinuating that the lizard doesn't respect the king or the palace. There are no emotions involved. To the lizard, the king walking in the palace garden is just another human walking among the rocks and flowers. We humans tend to assign emotional value to the social status of the individuals with whom we interact. Our bosses especially elicit emotional responses that tend to cause us to scurry into the rocks and hide. Showing respect is different than showing fear. God wants us to walk upright in all ways.

The proverb that I quoted at the beginning of this chapter goes on to say; "There are three things that are stately in their march, the lion which is mighty among beasts and does not retreat before any." One of my best friends in my life died in 2010 on July 10th. His name was Patrick Joseph McManus. "Pruney" or "P.J." as we called him was a lion. He was one of our greatest American mayors as mayor of Lynn, Massachusetts. I have to tell the world about P.J., he was the American dream. P.J. and I arrived at Bowdoin after very successful high school football careers in 1972. I met him the night before our first practice, so he and I headed for downtown

Brunswick, Maine to raise hell! He crowed on about how great he was going to be. "After a few years in the NFL, I plan on becoming the mayor of Lynn". He said, "Bobby, I'd rather live a day as a lion, then a lifetime as a lamb." This became our mantra. P.J. and I were from middle class families outside of Boston. We went to a college that was primarily for the wealthy. He and I received football scholarships; we took out student loans and worked as we attended Bowdoin. What we did not focus on was academics. We both partied hard and focused on football. But alcohol fueled intensity in our actions that hurt both of our lives and kept both of us from getting the most out of attending a fine school like Bowdoin. We both had lackluster academic records and both of us got into all sorts of mischief, none of which I will tarnish his reputation by sharing in this book. I was kind of like John Belushi in the epic film Animal House. I was the Warthog! Yes, you've purchased a book from a guy named Warthog! I leave the rest to your imaginations.

P.J. graduated and tried out for the Jets. He didn't make the team. But what happened to Pruney was he went to AA and quit drinking back in 1978, before it was trendy. It took me another 17 years before I went the same route. Pat went on to get his M.B.A., his law degree, become a C.P.A. and became Lynn's mayor for more than a decade. P.J. was on the U.S. Conference of Mayors and was instrumental in opening trade in China, the native home to four of his five adopted children. P.J. had a vision for himself that he never lost sight of; he had the tenacity of the badger, the industriousness of the ant, the

53

dedication to public service of the locust and courage beyond that of a lizard, he was a lion. P.J. had charisma; he was a total leader. He followed his heart and his God. His behavior and actions embodied all of these qualities and made him a lion for his lifetime. We should demand these qualities from a person before we make them a leader. Pruney was happy. I never saw him afraid. I loved him and miss him.

Fear usually expresses itself as anger, hatred and contempt. Weak leaders need cowardly followers. This is a vicious cycle. Take great care to pick your leaders, take great care to salute your followers. Do not allow strife in your workplace. This is the top guy's job! There is a way to overcome your propensity to experience a fear response when you interact with superiors. The same method should be employed when dealing with peers, subordinates and all sentient beings. The Dali Lama suggests that we look at each person that we interact with as though he/she were our mother, assuming that your mother and you have a good relationship. This is our responsibility to select what pair of glasses we look through. I have only met a few successful bosses who really don't value the input of, and engagement with, his or her subordinates. No boss appreciates making an error in decision, then hearing "I knew that was going to happen" afterwards. No good follower lets his or her boss fall in a hole, when they know where it is. We all know people who like that to happen to bosses and a few who actually facilitate this. Letting your boss make a mistake is irresponsible, disrespectful and lazy. These are the ants that we need to put under the magnifying glass. The employees who have something to say, but never do, need to stand up and say their piece. It feels good, and if it is true, kind and necessary, then karma will work on your behalf. You will be amazed how much respect you'll receive when you actively try to show the same amount of respect that you give to your mother, to each person that you encounter. This is a lesson for leaders and followers.

There you have it, the ant, the badger, the locust, the lizard and the lion. The character qualities these critters exude are behaviors that God sees as exceedingly wise. When you exercise these qualities as habits, then God will provide for you.

What does Solomon warn us about? The fool, the sluggard and the gossip! When you exercise these qualities as habits, you won't ever have a career. At best, you will have a job. But, you won't have the respect of the people that you work with. A fool is one who refuses to learn, a sluggard is one who refuses to work, and a gossip is one who wastes time talking about others. There is nothing in our Holy Bible that encourages these behaviors. There is nothing in any Holy writing that I have ever seen that doesn't say these traits are wrong. But unless a specific company rule is broken once, twice, thrice and a fourth time, nobody gets fired for being a gossip. Ok, I'll go with the need for fair progressive discipline. But is there a no sluggard rule at work? Is there an anti gossip policy at work?

The law of balance tends to eliminate the fools over and over again.

A fool is somebody who has done his job for 15 years in a dying industry, has kids to feed, but comes home each night and drinks beer and watches the television instead of taking advantage of continuing his education, working with his children or volunteering his time to better our world. But we'll have to watch his fat butt on the news complaining that life sucks, because his plant closed and he can't find a job. What does volunteering have to do with it? I don't think there should be any unemployment insurance unless there is work exchanged for it. There is graffiti to be washed off walls, potholes to fill and children of working people to watch. I have volunteered my whole life and the opportunities that I have been offered through doing so have been amazing. God rewards the work of your hands with success. If you are out of a job, volunteer and a job will find you! I really think it is our responsibility to learn a living while we earn a living as long as we live. Never before in the history of man has it been easier to get educated. With on line colleges, you tube, and the internet one can learn anything one wants right there in your home. But there is a type of fool who refuses to learn to respect, to follow, and to contribute; there is nothing on the internet to help this kind of fool. Fire them! Let them starve and die.

I won't give any examples of fools, sluggards or gossips by name, because they are all alive and they'd sue me. I will use fictitious names, genders and numbers, but true events. We all know who they are at our workplace. What we don't recognize is that our system of supervision and management provides a great deal of what I'll call forced idle time for managers if things run well, and firefighting is the order of the day when things go wrong. Both are a waste. Leaders and good managers don't waste time, they spend time. The areas where I see the most waste of time are supervision, middle management, sales, and engineering. HEY, that's the middle class! Is there a correlation between the in-effectiveness of this group of people and the disappearance of the middle class? Absolutely! They deserve to become extinct because they don't add value, thank you Charles Darwin.

Can you imagine being the engineer whose entire career rests on one simple corrugated box design, which didn't fundamentally change in close to four decades? Now hold on to your seats, there were actually 6 people assigned to engineer a cardboard box that never changed. Houses and cars were paid for and kids were fed by engineers who never changed anything! An old established food processing business was recently purchased. They had dozens of people in their quality control department, today there are less than ten! The new owners realized how much waste they had in this department and the beer still tastes the same, no quality has been compromised while their standards are still the highest in the world. The good ole boy network in this country costs us millions a year. The older and more established the company, the stronger the network of sloth. Organizations get so large that the hidden internal agendas become to maintain the status quo, don't rock the boat, and keep our jobs!

The businesses that I was blessed to lead tried to service these giant organizations by providing superior quality, flexibility and deftness with the minimum of inventory on their books. Our product quality was excellent, but not discernible to the untrained eye to see a difference from our competition's product. We delivered service levels that were unparalleled in the industry. We were fleet footed, these giant firms were too big to shake and jive in a world market where high stepping is necessary. We helped them compete.

Many of the excess people in these enormous companies are very likely not sluggards; they probably work very hard doing nothing of value. The redundancies and unnecessary tasks that these giants have can be attributed to a collective mind-set that creates tasks and jobs that don't really contribute to safety, work environment or profit. Corporations will blame government regulations and our litigious culture. The true collective goal becomes job security, not profitable growth. The result leaves us too many managers and too few leaders. These non value added jobs feel empty and expendable. This feeling of not being in on the real action produces mind chatter that leads to poor followership and feelings of insignificance. Everybody should stop reading right now and go watch the movie "Office Space". Although the characters may be slight exaggerations, there is more truth to this comedy than fiction. The reason it is so funny is because it strikes home to so many of us. In fact, the hero of the movie leaves and goes crazy when he can't find meaning in his work. Thank God in the real world that there are plenty of Hals, Bonnies, and Kens to keep businesses running. The problem with large companies is that people forget why they are there, why they work. People take ownership in the tasks that they perform. They don't really understand if these tasks are truly value added or destined to become obsolete. These folks may be great followers. They do what they are told, how they are told, and perform tasks perfectly that add no value to the organization's critical business agendas. When these businesses begin to lose money or are acquired, any decent consultant or industrial engineer can uncover waste, redundancy and non value added positions. These jobs, rightfully, are the first to go, regardless whether or not the person in the eliminated position is an ant or a slug. It is easier to eliminate a position, in a weak leader's mind, than to eliminate a person.

Let's step on the slugs and find value added tasks for the ants! A strong leader eliminates people, a manager eliminates positions. The greatest quality that a strong leader should demonstrate is compassion! Only with fearless compassion can one really know his workforce, because people will really show themselves when they know they are dealt with compassion at all times. Then and only then, can one really know which people it is truly fair to eliminate, when business conditions warrant, and only when business conditions warrant! Leaders should not socialize with their subordinates for this reason. It sucks to have to lay off a friend. To the manager, it's laying off six employees in the widget polishing department. To the leader, it's Jose, Yi, Abdul, Grace, Juan and Betty.

But what can the follower do about all of this? The lizard isn't aware that he is inside the Palace garden, he is only a lizard. The palace may be under siege, like a business that is about to be acquired. If you let negative mind chatter dominate your thinking, your performance and countenance will show it. One may ask, "Who cares about performance if this plant is going to be shut down?" God cares. As long as you are receiving a pay check, you are obligated to the Universe to do your best and bring joy to those who you work with. It is God that will sustain you throughout your entire fleshly experience, not the XYZ Corporation. James is my favorite New Testament writer, because he talks about work. The second verse in the first chapter says;"Consider it all joy, my brethren, when you encounter various trials, knowing that the testing of faith produces endurance."

Remember we are first and foremost human animals. I live in an animal paradise. I have great relationships with the bear, the many elk and deer, the moose family and the foxes that call my property home. But each day there is a life struggle drama that takes place in our little valley. The fox kills a rabbit, the coyotes take a fawn, the owl snatches the baby coyote and it goes on in my presence daily. We think that our sophisticated existence is very different, but over time it really isn't. I had a fox with babies in a den across the street; that mother fox worked like mad to feed those kits, she became gaunt and exhausted. She never stops, she doesn't know how to. In our life cycle we will have to face trials and tribulations, loss of jobs, loved ones, and health. Life isn't for wimps! James goes on to say in verse 12 "Blessed is a man who perseveres under trial; for once he has been approved, he will receive the crown of life, which the Lord has promised to those who love Him." In verse 19 James says, "This you know, my beloved brethren. But let everyone be, quick to hear, slow to speak and slow to anger: for the anger of man does not achieve the righteousness of God." There you go folks! Be quick to hear, listen and learn, be open to change. Be slow to speak because your words are precious and have power. Don't waste them on company gossip and the rumor mill. Be slow to anger because angry people lose! Keep your head. Keep working, XYZ Corp may not need you anymore, but God has things for you to do; volunteer, spend precious time with your family, indulge in your passions. Your passions point the way to your destiny. Anger is like a bucket with a hole, it carries nothing but the promise of emptiness. Losing your job is just like that mama fox that chased a ground squirrel yesterday into a hole under my barn; squirrel 1, fox 0. But she just kept on hunting; 38 minutes later I saw her with a chipmunk in her mouth...God provides! A government study was reported in 2010 on CNN that was aimed at understanding how the unemployed in America spent their time in 2009. The results are DISGUSTING! The #1 & #2 activities that increased were sleeping and watching television. There was no increase in education, exercise or volunteerism. You get what you deserve! But what you don't understand is that this collective force of negative energy, napping and watching television, is contributing to the unrest in the Middle East because this collective energy typically is angry, fearful and wasteful. Everything is connected.

Chapter 2
Judgment

"You are never free as long as you have to prove who
you are." Joyce Meyer

"Judge not, lest you be judged" is a common Christian
statement. People hate to be judged, yet if you lead
people in an organization, this is the most important part
of your job. For this reason, a chapter on judging is
essential for a book on leadership and followership. I
have asked for Divine guidance on this chapter to
convey truth, not prejudice and to not convey arrogance.

I am a news junkie and my first dose of it comes in the
form of Head Line News Morning Express. I have
watched this show or a version of it for a couple of
decades. Today is 12/3/12 and part of their news
broadcast stated that there were 3 major US
corporations, looking for employees. UPS had over
5,000 openings and had to offer bonuses to find
candidates. The primary reason experts gave for a lack
of people who are applying for these jobs is unemployed
workers are afraid to give up their unemployment
benefits for a risky seasonal job. It is easy for me to
judge these people as lazy, but afraid is a better
description. Truthfully there is probably a little of both
and rightfully so. Each person is going to do what is
necessary to feed their family. The risk of losing
benefits feeds into a fear of failure and when it's all said
and done most responsible people will opt for what they

perceive to be the surer source of income. But when we turn down work that we pray to come into our lives, God moves this opportunity elsewhere quickly. 5,000 people have a golden opportunity to get their foot in the door at a wonderful company like UPS and they'd rather sit at home, sleep and watch TV. In China there would be polite, orderly, lines of over 15,000 people to apply for these positions for a fraction of the pay their US counterparts are receiving. President Obama would rather condition his minions to wait for the government handout. I see that it's working. He's so smart! No wonder he wants to be ruler of the world.

The divine job of judging is not for the faint of heart, nor the cruel, nor for those who lack compassion. On the contrary, only the most compassionate people should lead and judge. Only people who have paid their dues of hard work over time should lead. A good leader works harder than his or her people, listens, seeks truth, enables his minions to contribute according to their abilities, is fair and sets standards of performance that exceed that of ALL of their competitors. Standards of performance that do not exceed your competition; WON'T! When our new Chinese boss gets here, our performance will either meet or exceed what they are used to, or we will be replaced, there will be no unemployment compensation for poor performers. In the mean time, we have an opportunity to judge ourselves and take corrective actions in our individual lives' to keep our future Chinese boss in China a little longer.

There are enormous differences between seeing truth, evaluating performance and judging. NEVER before in the history of man is it easier to see truth; surveillance cameras, GPS tracking and cameras on phones, automobiles and RF cards on your kids all give clarity where it was always fuzzy. Man keeps inventing ways to statistically evaluate behavior and performance to keep an aura of "judgment" out of discussions about personal value and contribution. Last but not least, lawyers make a living out of seeking injustices out of the judgments of businesses, employers, doctors and teachers. There will be punishment meted out if prejudice or unfairness is perceived. This leaves an environment that cripples true leaders and enables horrible performers to continue to pollute the work environments they inhabit with their negativity and sloth. In China this kind of poor performer could be hung! How are you going to deal with that EEOC?! OH! That's right! The agency won't stand a chance in a Chinese run government. Perhaps you will be able to get a job aborting babies when couples get pregnant after they already have one child. This is a common occupation in China. Every penny you send to China helps perpetuate their lifestyle over ours. How will you feel when your youngest gets taken by the state because you and your husband wanted a big family? Don't worry; they may let you pick which child you get to keep. The good news is that they'll put your remaining children to work close by in factories right here in America so Wal-Mart can exploit your children along with third world children. Last year America had 3.95

million people born and only 2.426 million people died. Your new Chinese government will simply do what works in China, forced abortions, 1 child limit and no old people plugged into things to keep them alive. They'll fix the imbalance with executions for people like me and those of us that just can't stop loving America.

Back in the old days, truth wasn't easy to see and perceived performance had as much to do with friendship as with actual contribution. Solomon wouldn't have needed to draw the sword if the brothel in which the two prostitutes and babies lived would have had 24 hour surveillance cameras. In that day one had to hear several sides of a story and "judge" based on many factors. But recordings, DNA and camera phones take the guesswork out of "he said; she said" anymore. Time clocks and computer tracking of output along with performance agreements based on goals help take the "friendship" out of evaluations. But our pendulum has swung too far in the direction of the science of evaluations in an attempt to replace judgment with a mathematical answer. Our entire human resource world has computerized the job application process so they don't have to actually read resumes or meet potential candidates before candidates are selected for interviews. There is no accounting for charisma, the #1 leadership prerequisite. Pizzazz can only be experienced face to face. This is done for efficiency and liability sake…the computer hired him, not me! Since most great leaders are somewhat revolutionary, the computer will spit them out in favor of the drones who comply all of their lives. The charismatic visionary or "path cutter" has to work outside of our corporate systems because the computers won't let them in anymore. What are left are layers of well meaning, hard working people who don't/won't rock the boat. Most human resource professionals wouldn't recognize charisma if it wore a sign, their role rarely requires it. Their job is to keep the company out of trouble. These layers of people produce reams of meaningless stuff that never contributes to profitability, but as long as they perform within the guidelines of their evaluations, they think that they contribute something important. Our Chinese bosses will quickly evaluate our contribution to profitability, regardless of our years of glowing performance evaluations, raises and promotions. Jobs devoted to safety, sales, human resources, environmental compliance and supervision are all at risk. There will be no EEOC, EPA or OSHA in America when we become the Western Republic of China. In North Korea they have a system of concentration camps for the families of individuals who disrespect the government which are not nearly as bad as the prisons that dissidents end up in. I'm sure something comparable will be provided for people who have made way too much money, contributing way too little value in this country when our conquerors' arrive. While we sit on our couches and surf the net for porn, our North Korean counterparts are busy taking target practice with our picture on the bull's eye and teaching their children to hate us because we are evil! Oh yes, they are starving while we anguish over the end of "Twinkies". They just set off their 3rd nuclear bomb!

We are so afraid to be judged, we want to protect our children from being judged. Judgment that isn't favorable hurts. If it is true and it hurts; it is good for you. We need to be truer to ourselves. This means that we need to put ourselves through American boot camp and rid our country of inefficient jobs, sloth and leadership that lacks integrity. We need to redefine the concept of work. If you can't find a job, you need to be thankful, educate yourself and volunteer. A job will find you. If you have a job, you need to be thankful and really judge yourself. As Uncle Sam would ask; "Are you all that you can be?" Are you really what you wanted to be when you grew up? Our new Chinese bosses will test us and match us to something they have deemed us fit for. Take the time today to keep that way of life from our shores. Do it yourself! The harder you are on yourself, the less likely anyone else will be hard on you.

The Jewish Laws that included the 613 commandments, clearly detailed sin and the recompense for that sin. Sacrifices were made on an Altar. Your thoughts, words and actions were compared to the list of acceptable and unacceptable actions. This was done constantly so behavior, and therefore performance, would steadily improve throughout one's lifetime as one repents from negative action and embraces positive choice. When God's will is expressed in writing and you understand it, you can easily judge your behavior against his expressed will. If you don't know His will, your choices will be manipulated by what the world deems right and wrong. The world longs for acceptance, God demands obedience. When we don't obey His word, even out of ignorance; the consequences will always end up negative as a learning tool. This keeps God constant and consistent. The Christian/Jewish/Muslim God is always judging. We just don't like it when His negative words to us come out of the mouths of another one of His human servants, especially our boss, coach, teacher, pastor, parents, or children. We immediately become defensive and usually argumentative. This slows down our change and our superior's agenda. Remember, we were hired to further our bosses agenda, not our own! Our boss has every right to express anger over our falling short of expectations that we make while interviewing. He or she has every right to warn us and replace us if we don't comply. To hell with what some government agency feels is fair. In the long run if your boss says you suck, you probably do. Your next employer will soon feel the same about you unless you change. It always works this way.

When we are free, we will still experience many of the things that enslaved people do, but we answer to God first, our earthly bosses or conquerors next. Only people and Satan enslave other people. It is not possible to live according to the direction in our Bible and not be a free man or woman. Even if one ends up in a Chinese run prison for doing something like writing this book it will be like Paul was in Rome; this would be a great way to die! Our president wants us to simply look the other way while we sell our world to China. We need to plan on fighting for our American freedom each and every day that we wake up and go to work. If more is required, be prepared to lay down our lives, so younger Americans can experience the lifestyle that we've had here in America. A new rule should be passed for nations contemplating war. The older citizens should serve first. Wars are fought by young people for old people's ideals. Let's require the age for enlistment to be 60 and see if we go to war. There is no freedom for a nation at war.

In the meantime ask yourself, are you really free? If you are on a constant mission to prove yourself to someone else, they are your captors. They imprison you in your bed at night, in your car on the way to work and all day long on the job. They judge you all day and night in your own mind. Therefore it is your responsibility to reprogram your own minds to keep this judge at bay. He is Satan, not your boss, teacher, coach or parent. Faith in God and study of His words are the first step in the reprogramming process.

In the meantime take all criticism seriously. For most people, it is very difficult to confront another human about poor performance or behavior. So when it happens, seek the truth in the complainers' words, they usually are based on truth. Understanding how hard it is to muster up the courage to confront someone about something, it's real. Listen and try to change regardless of who God decides to speak these words of truth through, the king or the pawn, it makes no difference, one should change and grow when one knows the criticizer's words align with God's will and our behaviors don't.

In my 47 years as a member of the American economic machine, I have had many roles. I had ownership in an executive recruitment firm and I was a business owner or operator for 31 years. I have interviewed and supervised thousands of people at all levels from PHD to ex-cons. I can quickly evaluate the potential of an interviewee for most positions, from sales to engineering to accounting and back, with an impressive level of accuracy as to long term success of a candidate. Like any job, if one does it all of the time, they gain skill, selecting people for a job is no different. One gets better at it with age and experience. I am an expert at picking people after dozens of failures. Solomon wasn't far off; it takes 1,000 men interviewed to find a good man. All hiring and firing requires judgment, both are as close to giving life and execution as we get without having a child or hanging someone. Both actions are as spiritual as they are economic. The person in charge of hiring and firing should have a direct hotline to God before either happens. The EEOC wouldn't like that!

When we take on a full time job with any organization, we enter into the spiritual realm of God's play pen. This happens with all covenants that we make; it is serious stuff. How we act and interact with the souls in this business is very important to God. The truth is more of your waking hours will be spent with your co-workers than with your spouse. This is a great place for God to judge us and He does, right at your work station day after day. The workplace is the birthplace of adultery, theft, bearing false witness, sloth, gossiping and coveting. The workplace is also home to thousands of violent acts a week in America, including murder. We may sit in church for an hour a week, but the real church is in your own home and at your place of business. Putting God's will into action at home and work, sets one up for a grand life. Falling short in either realm will add suffering to your life experience.

Many very successful television preachers have discussed the probability that we are approaching the final judgment of man in the form of a great seven year tribulation concluding with a huge world war centered in Israel followed by the return of Christ and His 1,000 year reign of peace. The entire Christian population has the Book of Revelations on their mind in this day and age. There is no greater power than faith and collective consciousness. We individually call this tribulation into existence when we sin or worry. We all have a role in this future. Our collective actions can bring healing or more suffering, never before in the history of man have our actions counted more to God. God understands ignorance and has great patience with the ignorant as long as He sees that the ignorance is being remedied with faith, work and study. He forgives us believing Christians but He doesn't keep us from experiencing the consequences of our sin. Because never before in man's history has man had such easy access to truthful information, God's patience with ignorance is wearing thin. All of the pieces of the Tribulation puzzle are on the table. We help assemble this puzzle when we sin. But the godless people of this world are all around the table putting each piece of the puzzle in its place. The godless, secular world loves the things in life that God hates. He's coming soon! According to the Book of Revelations He plans on killing over 4 billion people in 7 years; Go God! Git-er-done! How's that for judgment?

It says in the Bible that no man knows when this time of Tribulation will be, so it is our duty to act like it may be tomorrow to be on the safe side. Truth is it could be centuries away, what is more likely is that we could be the first dynasty on earth to be conquered without a battle being fought. The Chinese will defeat us by writing checks. The pen is mightier than the sword.

Regardless, we must balance our preparedness with enjoying in Christ every moment that we take breath. You show your love for God every day in your actions towards other people. Love your family and friends like it's always the last time that you'll see them. Make your top priority to understand how God wants to use you as His servant each and every morning. Then spend your day adding value to all of the lives that you transact with and you will find joy, employment and love. Your life's positive contribution will help keep the Tribulation at bay, the Chinese in China and food on your table. When one behaves this way, most people will judge you favorably.

Chapter 3

Wal-Mart

If something seems too good to be true, it probably is.
Anonymous

I struggle with writing this chapter because I don't want
to appear like a bitter old man. In my twenties I
promised that I wouldn't close my mind to progress like
my grandparents had seemed to. I had a full head of hair
and ideals. I lost the hair but I still hold to many ideals.
I have also been a lifelong student of China and frankly,
there is a great deal about pre Red Chinese culture that I
love. But the Chinese of today have endured half a
century of communist rule and this has all but eliminated
their hope for freedom of religion, freedom of speech
and the choice to procreate according to individual
belief. There are generations of people who have never
experienced having a sibling. China has become a
country of only children and abandoned baby girls. The
ideal that a society shouldn't grow beyond its ability to
sustain itself seems logical. China needed to put the
brakes on population growth in order to enable their
society to survive. Their economic growth needed to
significantly improve to accomplish this balance of
economic health to population levels. Today China is
experiencing the economic boom that America did after
the Second World War. The manufacturing tactics that
we employed in the forties and fifties, which precipitated
horrific working conditions, union growth and extreme
environmental pollution, are being used in China today

to fill the aisles of Wal-Mart, Target and Best Buy around the globe.

Our production workers and managers get paid enormously more than what we see in Chinese factories. Wal-Mart, GM, GE and all of the "American??" corporations who have invested heavily in China, have done a great thing from a global, humanitarian standpoint at the expense of American economic stability and national security. The perpetrators of the union/management nonsense that bloats our national cost structures while hamstringing efficiency efforts have nobody but themselves to blame. But all Americans are suffering as a result. A company cannot have a union and compete globally in the long run anymore.

There was a time in America when we needed unions. In the last century when OSHA, the EPA and the EEOC were in their infancy, unions ensured fairer pay, safer working conditions and justice in dispute. Do we really need unions anywhere in America today as these government agencies become more and more effective? The unions will have to move to China too, it will happen. In the meantime our American workers do their jobs in comfortable, safe working conditions and earn more in two hours than their Chinese counterparts earn all week.

We've created an organization called the Environmental Protection Agency which rightly insists that our factories don't pollute the environment. It is extremely expensive to comply with EPA standards and operate many key manufacturing processes. Pollution is so horrible in

China today that facemasks have to be worn while outside. People die regularly as a result of working unsafely with hazardous materials and the water is not safe to drink. Nobody knows how they dispose of their hazardous waste. But in America, our corporations are held accountable for their waste and this is expensive. If a company is claiming to be "Green" shouldn't that require a global perspective to be truly green? American corporations that manufacture products in China while knowingly polluting the environment beyond what our scientists have established as safe should be called on the global carpet for this. Pollution does not honor national boundaries.

The treatment of laborers in China by those in leadership would make Stephen Covey cringe. There is zero tolerance for dispute, poor quality workmanship, low productivity, or absenteeism. Feeling warm and fuzzy in a discrimination free workplace is a non priority in China. China brings a whole new meaning to "employment at will"; you will do what you are told or you won't be employed.

Retirement savings are invested throughout one's life in the American stock markets. We seek to invest in companies that offer the highest and safest return on our money. This represents businesses with the highest profitability. Wal-Mart, GE, GM and other well run American corporations buy their products and services from the least cost suppliers of these products and services to maintain these profit levels. These corporations are forced to buy at the lowest prices in order to maximize profits to attract investors like you and me. Indeed, they have honed the resource strategies available today to turn the job of purchasing into a fine science. Every penny is accounted for; only the least cost producers survive.

Those that shop to maximize each dollar, buy items that have a quality level that is acceptable at the lowest cost possible. Responsible people look for the best bargains to feed their families. This is what smart shoppers do. But should we buy blood diamonds because they are cheap? Would you buy a toaster from a company if you could see that a 16 year old girl that they employ slaves 12 hours a day in 100 degree polluted heat for $9 a day to make it? If it was your 16 year old daughter and the company was in your American town, you'd go to the authorities and report it.

China is the answer to rising manufacturing costs today, yesterday it was Mexico, and tomorrow it may be Africa. Wal-Mart is the dominant global outlet for companies that pay the lowest earthly wages to people working in deplorable working conditions for companies that pollute the environment at will. Today these companies are in China, India, Pakistan and other third world countries.

When we buy from these countries, we say yes to pollution and human slavery. Buying a lawn mower made in China says that you don't care about your brothers and sisters who labor in places and ways we would forbid here in America. We perpetuate their situation when we buy a mower made in China instead of one made in Colorado.

The conundrum we face is; do we focus on raising our Chinese brethren out of squalor at the expense of our quality of life, or focus on protecting our middle class at the expense of the quality of life of third world slaves? Are we truly going global? Then let's require a level playing field for pollution controls, working conditions and human rights. Let the economics for labor balance itself out and say goodbye to the middle class in America and Europe as we know it. This will enable more people to live at a higher level of lower class than ever before worldwide.

Which is God's will? Is it not His whole world? Would God prefer that we raise the standard of living for a billion poor people by 200% while lowering the standard of living for a couple of hundred million rich people by 20%? If so; our corporate leaders are following God's will by investing in China! Would God not drool at the prospect of bringing a billion souls to Christ? Maybe that is the master plan. What does that mean for those of us left in America? Is this what corporate America and our president are up to? Bringing the standard of living up for the majority of the world while paring back nations whose lifestyles are steeped in excess and luxury seems in line with God's word.

Does this mean that a Christ centered American should forego patriotism for more global, humanitarian endeavors and efforts? We are "One Nation under

God"; China is not. Is it our evangelical duty as Christians to expand into China at the expense of our American way of life?

Does God want to meter out some punishment to America for ignoring Him? Is God trying to teach His spoiled children to share?

Those of us left here in America need to wake up and go to work. We need to be thankful and hopeful, but we need to step the pace up even more. We need to understand that every time we buy an item from a third world nation, we move ourselves closer to becoming one. Each day 4 billion dollars are lost from America to China. At last count China owned 18% of America and growing. America only owns 23% of America! We need to put every able bodied American to value-added work, job or not. We need to eliminate wasteful work, stop buying stupid stuff and learn to speak Chinese. We need to stop giving money to people for not working! If they starve it is their choice, always! The Bible says; He who does not work, neither should he eat.

Only a world war or enormous natural disaster can stop the economic takeover of America by China in the near future. Kudos to Apple Computer, they are investing in the United States for the first time in decades next year, kudos to Michigan for changing its labor laws. We need to take drastic measures now to avert a total takeover soon. The important wildcard that we have no idea as to how it will play out is our freedom of religion.

MAKE NO MISTAKE! Our Chinese counterparts do not believe in our God. God's will does not factor in the decisions made in China. When the billion people who conquer us believe that we are guided by ancient agricultural mythology, our freedom to worship may be put at great risk. When we buy items made by Godless people, we support their agendas at the expense of God fearing people's economic welfare. This rapidly changing world may render national patriotism obsolete as technology steadily makes the world a smaller place. But God will NEVER become obsolete!

It very well may become un-cool to be a national patriot in the near future regardless of which country one hails from. Indeed, it may become illegal to discriminate worldwide based on nationality. Those standing up as a patriot may be regarded like racists are today. Us old fashion Americans had better wake up and smell the tea too. "Leave it to Beaver", Ozzie, Harriet and the "Partridge Family" do not represent the ideal American family anymore. Father may know best, but he had better call mother at the office for permission and say it in Mandarin. We don't need to ask father anymore anyway, we have Google.

In light of the fact that the merging of China and America is well underway and not about to slow down, our leaders need to be straight with us about how they think that this will play out. No matter what the truth is, we need to individually prepare in the same way. We need to seek God's will for us each day asking Him how we can best serve Him today. Then we have to read

God's word, pray and get up and go to work for His purposes. Jobs will come and go, but His work for us is steady, interesting, ever changing and truly fulfilling. No person needs to be represented by a union when God is the boss. If we as individuals follow what God's word directs to in our work, He will peacefully sustain us through the loss of an American identity and lead us to our new global identity. As long as we are identified as one of God's Holy anointed children; who cares what national identity we need to align with? The only time we should care and consider war is if we are forced to abandon our faith in God.

Even when we lean towards apocalyptic thought, the remedy of believing in God, asking God for our individual assignment, praying and carrying out His work each day and avoiding; sloth, gossiping and foolishness, puts one on the Rapture list for sure. Therefore, these individual actions that we need to take will work for us whether we are simply facing another recession, a national take over, or the Tribulation, taking the same God-centered approach, is doing the right thing!

No man knows when that time will be, not even the Son, only the Father. When a nation holds one billion souls who don't know Christ, there seems to be a whole lot more work to do before we begin the Tribulation. Our Lord has told us Faith, Hope and Love are the keys to the kingdom, the greatest of these is love. But Hope is a big hitter too and having strong hope for a great future is absolutely essential for having one. Like the ant, expect to live productively many years past your biological life expectancy. There is no greater demonstration of hope for a future than to work tirelessly like the ant to provide for future generations because they KNOW future generations will exist. There may not be future generations of Americans, but there will be future generations of Christians. Which is more important to you?

What about non believing Americans? The need to lead with integrity and follow with devotion still applies. Take belief out of the equation and these Americans are still competing with Chinese, Indians and Pakistanis for the same jobs. Working harder for less will still be required. Preparing to live happier with less material possessions and a lower level of personal freedom is a wise way to prepare for the future for all of us, believer or not. Those who are capable of succeeding will really have to have the goods to make it. Those that currently perform averagely and live in our middle class will either have to step up the performance and value to your employers or get ready to live in a rented apartment instead of a mortgaged home. Those that live in our middle class and work like animals to make ends meet, have tougher roads ahead as the cost of living continues to rise and incomes continue to drop. Working really, really hard is better than fighting a war. Working really, really hard is better as a free American, than a captured slave.

Chapter 4

How we work

"While practices are situationally specific, principles are deep, fundamental truths that have universal application. They apply to individuals, to marriages, to families, to private and public organizations of every kind. When these truths are internalized into habits, they empower people to create a, wise variety of practices to deal with different situations." Stephen Covey

This chapter is about work habits or practices. But before we talk about how we work, we need to understand how we think. When I speak of mind chatter, I am referring to that internal dialogue that keeps playing over and over in our mind. I think that for purposes of discussion some paradigms need to be understood. As a psychology student at Bowdoin and early in my career as a supervisor I was educated in an approach to understanding the development of the mind known as Transactional Analysis (TA).

TA is a neo Freudian theory of personality which dovetails off of Freud's concept of Id, Ego and Super-ego and was created by Eric Berne in the 1950's. Berne combined elements of psychoanalysis, cognitive and humanist approaches to understand the mind chatter and emotional programming that may have occurred in our past which affects our lives today. The very concept of ego originated with Freud, but Berne put Freud's theories into a workable model that enables one to have insights to human behavior and thus, help one find the magic buttons to push to cause action in someone else. The definition of motivate is; move-to-act.

When we communicate, this involves everything; listening, talking and non-verbal cues all send a message. We are responsible for how we communicate. All communication is defined as a "Transaction" by Berne. When we analyze each transaction we try to understand which dynamic of the Child/Parent/Adult component of the speaker's personality is dominant in what is being transacted. We also listen inside ourselves to understand which dynamic of the personality is being aroused when we receive the communication before we respond.

Berne says that we have three primary components of our personality. The first stage of the mind he defines as the "Child". This corresponds to the concept created by Freud called the Id. The first stage of mental development involves very basic need satisfaction. In essence, the goal of the "Child" is to find pleasure and avoid pain. This is what moves the baby to act; cry, laugh etc. The "Child" seeks to have fun as we develop mentally while we grow. The "Child" part of our personality also seeks to avoid pain, criticism, embarrassment, work and betrayal. The mind develops and the other two dynamics of the personality grow accordingly.

The second component of our personality that comes into play after birth is developed through the interaction of our parents with our lives. We begin our mental programming at birth by our parents. We have no power but crying at this stage, so the parents control everything else. Appropriately, the dynamic of the personality that has a goal of control is called by Berne; the "Parent", this corresponds to Freud's Super-ego. The goal of the "Parent" is to control others. Often if we micromanage somebody, we must ask; are we trying to guide this person or control this person? If our actions and words are being received as controlling, they are. If I perceive your actions and words as controlling, my tendency will be to respond in defense. This defensive response will originate from the "Child" in me that wants to avoid pain.

As the dynamics between the child and parent continue, the final stage of development of the mind begins to grow. Freud called this component the Ego; Berne calls it the "Adult". The Goal of the "Adult" is to be competent. The three components then are the "Parent", "Adult" and "Child", usually depicted as three circles side by side for analysis purposes. During TA training everyone takes a personality profile test that indicates which component of the personality we operate from predominantly or rarely etc. This helps us to understand ourselves and points direction to areas that may need attention and improvement. But this book isn't about TA and there is plenty of great stuff on the internet for those who want to learn more. This discussion is for the purpose of understanding my paradigms. I have used discussions on TA throughout my career with my teams. What I want to underscore is that as a boss we must be careful not to treat our subordinates like naughty, untrustworthy children. When we do, we get a response that comes from the pain avoiding natural "Child" in them.

Our goal in all communications should be to interact as "Adults" to allow the emergence of the pleasure seeking natural "Child" in all of us so we can live like adults and enjoy life like children. If we obsess about proving to others that we are the most competent one; we are egotistical or "over-Adult". When we take credit for our accomplishments instead of giving praise to God, we are egotistical or irreverent. But to be consistently and humbly competent is okay. We love feeling competent. When our boss treats us like children, this feeling gets threatened. If it occurs regularly one loses the fire to work like an ant. This is a major threat to positive performance for the entire organization, family or our nation.

When our business is in danger it is difficult to remain a good ant, when we are not respected for being an adult, we become unruly, pain- avoiding children. As a good person of God and a good follower, we need to take responsibility for not acting like a spoiled "Child"; we need to be children of God and act like "Adults" regardless of how the Universe is treating us at this time. All three components of our personality can become predominant and nothing to excess is good, if we need to control everything or if we take nothing seriously then we allow mind chatter to spring forth from these dynamics of our personality and negative results occur.

Mind chatter is like the bubbles in a beer. These bubbles just spring forth from no particular place in the glass, and rise to the surface. Joel Osteen says that these thoughts are like channels on your television, you may not be able to choose what is on each channel, but you do have the mental remote channel changer and can select which show to pay attention to. If our boss criticizes us in front of a customer, we feel anger and embarrassment. If we play this channel over and over we will still feel the same way even if weeks have passed. This is non-motivating and it is our responsibility to change the channel. When we congregate with peers and voice these feelings of malcontent, this will become contagious and damaging. Have you really understood why you were criticized in the first place? Or are you behaving like your teenager? Are you killing the messenger of God's voice over and over again in your mind chatter?

I want to share some very real examples of fictitious middle managers who may have once worked hard, earned very respectable wages, but chose to be both bad employees and non-followers. The rank and file; customer service reps, secretaries, factory workers, health care workers; the people who "Move the Rock" see this everyday in American businesses and keep their mouths shut to keep their jobs. The examples represent people who lack the basic work ethic, courage and integrity that enable chronically successful people to stay successful. To be fair I included examples of how we may not understand that what may look like play to the rank and file, may actually be very hard work. It isn't always easy to see what actions actually have productive value to your organization. Neither side should be quick to judge, it is time to understand.

This is a story of Fred. Fred was a computer nerd in a day when there were few. His behavior was basically lazy at work, home or at play. He was a chronic complainer and a cynical person most of the time. But in the 80's when the computer revolution was in full swing, Fred had skill sets that were marketable and he landed a job with a manufacturing firm to install their new computer system. This is a horrible task for those of you who have gone through systems implementation or change over.

Fred did a good job of setting up the system and a thorough job of programming and populating the required fields that got the system up and running. This took 18 months. After the installation was complete and the system was trouble shot, the required tasks for Fred dropped by 82%! He was named the Information Systems Manager, given a raise and lauded for a job well done, but he had 82% less work to do and his boss didn't know his role well enough to fill that 82% with value added work.

Fred became a master at causing problems to fix them to show his worth and he spent the remainder of most days smoking cigarettes and going from office to office and gossiping. He attended every meeting but rarely contributed. He knew which reports were needed and he was diligent about making sure his system performed. There was no internet in those days or he would have spent his time surfing the web and calling it work. This went on for years and the company grew beyond its management team and I was called in to address inefficiencies in their production and engineering departments. The first thing that my work sample study showed was that Fred worked less than 35% of the time and I gave him credit when he attended meetings that he didn't contribute to or was documented as on the phone. He loved to tell me of how hard he worked 9 years ago implementing his system and how it never failed. Again I would have to turn the conversation around to the truth that he wasn't contributing today. If he simply stopped coming to work, nothing would skip a beat. I would promote Diane, the department secretary, to the position of manager at half the pay (and at fair market value) of Fred. She did all of the work in the department anyway. She would get a 30% raise for doing the same job she was doing. We would save $112,000 a year in salary and fringes and more importantly all of the people Fred wasted time with would not have that daily interruption and his negative impact on morale would be resolved.

I explained this to Fred and I gave him two options. He could assume the shipping supervisors role and fill that 82% of his day with work. Or he could be the night computer operator, keep his title and pay and keep out of my sight. But either way his performance and workload were going to change or he was going to become a history lesson.

Fred did what most people like Fred do. He spent weeks complaining about me. He was going to sue and he began documenting every meeting that I had and every questionable thing everybody else "got away with". What he did NOT do was come to work each day and do the job he was extremely overpaid to do. He was not given a raise and he was "red circled". Meaning his salary was so far above the corporate range for his position that he wouldn't be receiving a raise until he got promoted or hell froze over. His performance was horrible and his review reflected that. He firmly believed that if things didn't go wrong in his department, then his performance was acceptable. I insisted that I wanted him to actually physically work at doing tasks that we needed as a business. He took it to a lawyer. He did not change his behavior or performance. At the end of the first quarter, Fred was given a warning about spending too much time in other people's offices and noted that none of his goals were met for the first quarter. These were goals he set and gave me. He refused to sign the warning. The next month his performance and behavior continued to slide. Yes, true to my form, I addressed that with him and put him on probation.

His wife called me and told me he was drinking heavily and very depressed but they needed this job because they had kids in college. For legal reasons I couldn't talk to his wife. His drinking did what drinking does, made things worse and his attendance crossed the line of acceptable and Fred was terminated for cause. The department of Employment denied his claim and his charge of age discrimination with the EEOC was dismissed as no probable cause. All Fred had to do was come to work on time, do what he was told to do and paid to do.

Fred couldn't get out of his pain avoiding "Child". Nor could he stop his bad work habits anymore than he was able to quit smoking. He couldn't accept that I was 20 years his junior. He didn't have any work to do in his old role that had died nine years ago. It's a shame that my predecessor allowed him to not contribute for nine years but they were drinking buddies. Fred and his boss exemplified the "Good Ole Boy" network. Fred was not able to follow. He was not able to accept criticism of any sort. Nor would he look at where he could actually add value, contribute and keep his excessive salary. Instead he wanted to do the tasks that he wanted to do. He felt his age and seniority entitled him to it.

Fred loved to gossip. He was addicted to it and it cost him his livelihood! To Fred, his 8 hours at work was a social thing. Is there a rehab for gossips? Fred is not the exception, he is the rule when it comes to adults over 30 whose performance or behavior warrants progressive discipline. They just can't get out of the "Child" blame game. The exception is a person who listens and works to change. Fred never once looked in the mirror and said; "I am responsible for losing my job because I refused to do what my boss told me to do." He refused to follow as he was paid to.

One of the most difficult jobs to be successful at is sales representative. Regardless of the product or service that one sells, the same skill sets are required to be consistently successful. Nothing happens in business until you sell something. The single most critical positions in any business are on the sales team. A great sales professional is worth more than their weight in gold. There are several key behavioral characteristics that successful sales people need and unfortunately, some of these personality traits conflict with one another. There are two types of successful sales people, closers and servicers. Actually to be a well rounded sales professional one needs to be both. However, the closer is the more valuable. The first personality stereotype that one thinks of, when thinking of sales professionals, is that they are people oriented. Sales people try to please constantly, they like to be liked and typically they are very sensitive to criticism. However, it takes a person who can handle rejection over and over again yet can still come in and keep that up-beat enthusiasm working. In the packaging industry we used to expect to win 10% to 15% of the quotes for new business that we submitted. That means 85% are rejected. When courting large companies like Kraft or Motorola, one can expect to spend a couple of years to get them to switch to a new, qualified supplier. This takes incredible tenacity and patience and a willingness to be ready to strike when opportunity presents itself.

For the typical sales rep, opportunity typically comes in the form of a personnel change in the purchasing department or a new product release or a quality/cost problem with an existing supplier. When these opportunities present themselves, the successful rep is prepared and ready to seal the deal. This preparation takes discipline and energy. The unsuccessful rep, takes people to dinner, plays golf a lot, but always has some "external excuse" for not closing the deal.

The Chinese philosopher Chuang Tzu tells a tale of a fisherman prince, in Burton Watson's translation, the story is told that "Prince Jen made an enormous fish hook with a huge line, baited it with fifty bullocks, settled himself on top of Mount K'uai-chi, and cast with his pole into the eastern sea. Morning after morning he dropped the hook, but for a whole year he got nothing. At last a huge fish swallowed the bait and dived down, dragging the enormous hook. It plunged to the bottom in a fierce charge, rose up and shook its dorsal fins, until the white waves were like mountains and the sea waters lashed and churned. The noise was like that of gods and demons and it spread terror for a thousand li. When Prince Jen had landed his fish, he cut it up and dried it and from Chip-ho east, from Ts'ang-wu north, there was no one who did not get his fill. Since then the men of later generations who have piddling talents and a penchant for odd stories all astound each other by repeating the tale."

"Now if you shoulder your pole and line, march to the ditches and gullies, and watch for minnows and perch, then you'll have a hard time ever landing a big fish. If you parade your little theories and fish for your superiors to see, you will be far from the Great Understanding. So if a man has never heard of the style of Prince Jen, he's a long way from being able to join with the men who run the world."

Prince Jen was the kind of sales person who lands a multimillion dollar account. This kind of big fish can employ hundreds of people for years. This kind of salesmanship creates security. The people who march to ditches and gullies are those that go through the motions of trying to sell something. They will make 50 calls every day to phone numbers belonging to people that they don't have a relationship with. They leave a message on the answering machine and consider it a sales call, consider it a job well done. These people walk into a lobby unprepared and call the purchasing department and ask to talk to someone. However, this very rarely succeeds at getting anything accomplished, yet they will climb back into their company car and consider it a sales call. These people don't know how to go about selling. Sales people who watch for minnows and perch are those sales people who spend too much time on accounts or activities that pay too little. This can also include sales people who don't know who to contact. If you parade your little theories and fish around talking big, you will tend to look like a fool to people of understanding. Your little fish shows you are not a skilled fisherman, and therefore your theories are not worthy of being paraded. This kind of sales person tends to be the first at the bar during cocktail hour, bragging on about nothing to anyone who will listen. A successful salesperson may be at that bar, but he or she will likely be entertaining a customer or potential customer and not their bar buddies. The successful sales person listens, the unsuccessful sales person, brags.

The word "tip" actually means "To Insure Performance". Waiters may receive a wage below minimum because they typically receive tips. We pay an amount that is usually a percentage of the bill. Most of us simply cough up 15-20% of the bill. This should be based on how well the waiter or waitress did their job. The rationale is that requiring the wait person to perform before he receives his pay will motivate this person to work harder or smarter. Sales people tend to work on commission for the same reason. There are as many commission plans as there are products to be sold. Properly structured incentive systems work for everybody. Any job can have an incentive pay system tailor made for it that rewards behaviors which contribute to profitability. Most sales commission plans boil down to a percentage of the revenue dollars for a designated period. This can include adjustments for new business or products. Expenses may be paid separately or considered an employee responsibility. One may not allow commission to be paid if the account goes beyond 90 days as a receivable. There are a million ways to skin this cat. The important thing for this conversation is that most sales people work on incentive. During their first year as an employee, it is highly unlikely that one can earn enough right out of the gate. Because of this most sales people begin work at a salary that will be gradually reduced over time because their work should yield sales that pay commission.

Usually somewhere between 12 to 18 months one expects that the new sales person be well on their way to earning a living above their temporary starting salary with the commissions that they have earned by the sales they've closed. Accordingly, their starting salary is then either stopped or significantly reduced. If the sales person has not brought any business in over 12 months, he or she probably isn't going to produce the level of sales needed to support their salary.

Many times these people can prove to be excellent servicers. Often when a new sales rep joins a firm or an existing rep takes over an account, they may inherit a relationship that requires a significant amount of handholding. Only an involved sales manager knows how their reps spend their time. Then management has to determine how many service people they can afford to carry with the number of closers that the business has. As the business leader the thing to really pay attention to is new business development. Your organization should respond to your customers needs once they are established customers. Your salesman should be back on the lake fishing. If you have a salesperson who hasn't hooked a fish in 18 months, they won't perform on incentive. They probably are unskilled and undisciplined. They need to be tossed into the sea. We call these people 18 month wonders. When one advertises to hire an experienced sales person, the number of resumes that show patterns of employment

that last 12-18 months is astonishing, the reasons that
they give for needing to switch employers every 18
months tends to follow similar patterns as well. These
tend to be people who brag of little fish and theories.

I have found that a lack of tenacity and self discipline is
the number one and two reasons people fail in sales.
People can work very hard for 12 hours a day and not
accomplish anything if they are not disciplined enough
to plan their work and work their plan. Good mentoring
when one starts out can be invaluable when learning
how to plan and what to do. One can have horribly long
hard days putting out fires instead of planning and
managing well enough to keep fires from happening in
the first place. The problem, due to the sensitive egos of
most sales people, is they tend to do tasks that get them
complimented and avoid tasks that tend to get them
rejected. Servicing a client very well gets all sorts of
kudos when the job gets done. But who is out there
beating the bushes for new business while you're busy
kissing butt. It is those tasks that get one rejected which
eventually pay the greatest commission.

The worst thing one can do is pay commission for a
service rep if they didn't land the business. Pay them
well but reserve the big payouts for new business
development. The other short fall with inexperienced
sales people is that they just quit too early. They don't
follow up enough, they stop making calls too early in the
day or in the relationship, they quit being enthusiastic.
They begin to look for a new job after 12 months
because they know they will be let go soon for not

producing, so they collect pay for their own job search! And the 18 month wonder moves on, always in sales never selling anything. Good sales people who work for good companies with fair incentive systems tend to not write resumes. They don't make excuses; they overcome obstacles. A sales person with a resume in his or her car isn't selling anything but themselves.

It is so incredibly easy for outside sales people to not work. The blessing of freedom can become a curse that spells failure to many well intentioned sales people. The tasks of being a master sales person are so diverse and complicated that it takes at least 3 years for a talented, likable person to become competent if they accept quality education and guidance while they work hard. If they follow well!

People who are master sales professionals make gobs of money. It was not unusual for my best sales reps to make more money each year than I did. I happily paid them their reward because they kept the plant running and provided jobs for our workforce. I am not a master sales man; I am a master factory jockey. It took me decades to become masterful at manufacturing management. I dedicated my life to learning how to become a better manufacturing executive each year. To be a master craftsman at anything takes a lifetime of learning and performing. This requires intelligent use of time. There is a great deal of forced idle time in sales and management.

I helped our sales manager from the ranch as she had a sickness in her family, so I attended a conference of cattle ranchers and managed a booth that had an exhibit advertising our many services. During the day there was an ebb and flow of potential customers. From 9:00 till 10:25 we didn't have any traffic. But I had to be at the booth waiting. This is forced idle time and it happens to us all. There were really no other tasks that I could effectively do during that waiting time. Or was there? Absolutely there was. I networked with the other exhibitors and I actually generated more leads from this than I ended up getting from the ranchers. I also filled the time with a variety of follow-up tasks. The rep who worked two booths over did nothing but wait for somebody to stop by. We both probably got paid the same. He looked bored and sad, I had a blast! The difference is that in one case the fox initiates a hunt, in the other case the fox is waiting for his prey to come to him.

The amount of money and time that companies spend each year on entertainment is staggering. The costs of alcohol, golf and hunting to our company, was ridiculous. But a ton of business gets done on the golf course or at the nineteenth hole. The same can be said for bars and strip clubs. Great sales people build relationships and nurture these relationships by understanding the buyer and attending to his or her needs and passions. When there are no company policies in place, and enforced, to ensure that out-of-ethics behavior doesn't result between the buyer and the seller, you can be sure that lines will be crossed.

Companies like Kodak rotate their buyers so that relationships don't cloud business judgment. The kind of lines crossed include; kickbacks, fake expense reporting, providing customers with drugs, prostitutes or other illegal gifts. All things that God thinks are wrong. These crossed lines cost American businesses billions of dollars a year and invites God's curse to these businesses in the long run.

Entertaining for business is as American as apple pie. Unfortunately this is also part of the Chinese business mindset. Corruption is older than Jesus. This won't stop unless we make it a priority. The more "third world" a country is; the higher level of corruption there is to be expected. Most people question when businessmen and politicians are found to be jetting to exotic resorts for golf, sun and surf. But what really happens on these junkets can make or break a business or a country. Business managers spend hours at exotic places and rarely leave the conference rooms, executives close deals that employ thousands for decades. Conversely Governors that "walk the Appalachian Trail", in South America, cause a call to question the integrity of everybody that travels for "business".

I had to meet with a customer in Ensenada, Mexico once. I traveled with the Customer Service Rep who handled the account and we met the Salesman, Robert, who landed the account and our customer's Corporate Buyer in San Diego. Then we all drove down the scenic ocean highway to the manufacturing operation. The only difference was that the Customer Service Rep and I traveled in a Toyota Corolla and Robert drove our customer in a Jaguar convertible. After we met with the customer's manufacturing team in Ensenada we took the entire team out to dinner at a cost of over $2,500. Robert took the entourage out for drinks until 2:00 that morning at an additional cost of over $1,000. That team in Mexico loved to see Robert coming. We spent over $50,000 a year entertaining that customer. But with annual sales of $6,000,000 at a profit of 12.8%, one can see it was worth the Jag and $3,500 nights. During dinner no business was discussed, it was all about building lasting friendships. To most of the people on the team in Mexico, having dinner at the restaurants that we chose, was way out of their range of affordability. This was a very special event for them and made more so when we invited them to bring their spouses. The expenses may seem an extreme extravagance to our own factory laborers, but we wouldn't have kept the business, and they wouldn't have had jobs, had we not forged those relationships. I can say that Robert is a master at his craft. He makes several hundred thousand dollars a year and spends a hundred grand a year entertaining, but he sells over $12,000,000 a year in product. That's enough to employ over 50 people! He understands the style of Prince Jen. To the untrained eye it would appear that he spends most of his time jetting to the best golf courses in the world, eating at the finest restaurants and having a grand time of play. But Robert works all of the time and there is very little he won't do to close a deal. He has to be watched so the lines that he crosses don't come back to bite us, but he is working with every drink he buys, every game of golf he plays, every dollar he lets our customer put in a G string, and every bite of lobster. After he lands an account, he tends to be horrible at servicing it because he is after another big fish. He is driven by money and our incentive system pays more for new customers. He expects the customer service team and factory to support his customers once they are hooked. Many sales people wrongfully indulge too much time and energy in service after the sale because it's easier work. I had a boss who says that a great sales rep is like a motorboat on a smooth lake, it goes fast, gets a smooth ride, but causes a big wake. Those left to support the sales rep get the rough water.

In contrast, I had another rep, named Debbie, who we promoted into sales because she was a great marketing manager. She inherited a sizable account along with some smaller pieces of business from a rep that left the company. She grew the large account significantly each year because she handled them like fine china. Her tactics were geared at getting all of each of her customer's business, as opposed to opening new accounts. Debbie was loved by the people in the organizations that she sold to. She made friends with everybody, from the receptionist to the president. This one customer became a several million dollar account through her efforts. However she never actually opened an account with us in over 5 years as a sales person. There were three contributing factors that kept her from acquiring new business; 1) she was paid on the same commission plan as the salesman in the first example, but she had already surpassed her own personal financial goals by tens of thousands of dollars a year, 2) she couldn't tolerate rejection, and 3) her personal life problems kept her from being free enough to really spend the time necessary to grow as a professional of any kind. She did a fantastic job with her one big customer and kept her other accounts happy through her personal involvement. When people met her, they figured her to be in sales, she was a schmoozer. She had several banner years earning commission on business that she serviced, and stupidly, she upgraded all dimensions of her life. But businesses move and change over time, eventually all of her accounts left the States or the products that we supported, became obsolete. After seven years she lost her customers and her job because she couldn't open new business. She lacked self discipline in all areas of her life and eventually her work week dwindled to about 25 hours a week. But because she was an outside sales person, she wasn't easy to supervise and attending to her personal problems often took priority over working to drum up new business. She did what was needed to be done each day to keep her customers contented then her personal agenda was attended to. This happens all the time, all over the country. From the outside looking in, she was a very successful person. But she became a fool and a sloth, more than she was an ant or a locust, and the Universe kept its balance. She needed supervision. This happens by default when one works inside, but who is watching when you're an outside salesman other than God? If one doesn't really believe that He is watching, then He really doesn't make a good substitute for a supervisor.

Most sales managers don't like conflict and confronting a thirty something year old sales professional about work ethic and effort, without concrete evidence, rarely gets any other response but denial or deflection. Our country is loaded with salesman who cannot sell. When a sales professional is both a competent closer and servicer, they get promoted into sales management. When they are great at both, they go to executive management.

Debbie was a successful marketing manager. This is why she was given the opportunity that she had hoped for in sales. She earned it with being a great team player and hard work. She was charged as hell to go to work each day. As the commission checks grew, she correctly connected the dots between customer growth and personal income. She relentlessly went after every opportunity at each customer like she was supposed to and this broadened our product base as it increased our total sales, everything was good. Her pay actually tripled from when she was a marketing manager. She bought a bigger house, she bought her son a new car and she went deeper in debt. Debbie had more money than she ever dreamed that she would make. She actually wasn't motivated by the incentive system any more like Robert was. She made more than enough for her personal expectations. Robert never made enough. This happened for two years and life was good. But she started getting massages and going to beauty spas. She never had a manicure in her life until her second year in sales, now she had a weekly appointment. She had a teenage son who was starting to get into trouble and as a result she began going to lawyers and counselors. Then in her fourth year in sales, her number two customer moved their work to China. This represented $2,000,000 a year in sales or $60,000 in her annual income. Instead of replacing the time that she used to devote to servicing this customer by spending time finding new business, Debbie became harder to find. Based on my work samplings she was already not working a full week before this customer left for China. Her lifestyle had changed and now she didn't have the means to support it anymore. Which in turn led to more legal problems, this took even more time away from her job. She wasn't following anything other than her tail every day. Her whole life had gotten away from her. When this happens to an employee, it always affects their work performance. It happens to all of us at one time or another in our lives. When one lives on commission, one doesn't have the option to not perform like people on salaries do.

Debbie's Sales Manager let her down by not confronting her more about her work habit changes before they became new habits. He was a good salesman and a manager, but not a strong leader. But she was warned. If she was a good follower she would have made changes after one meeting about performance. We wanted her to change back to the Debbie she was, the one that her co-workers liked. We weren't asking her to become something that she wasn't capable of.

We actually began discussing performance with her towards the end of her third year as a sales rep. We noticed that she became unreachable more often and rumors had it that her new lifestyle was being cultivated during company time. She used her forced idle time to do personal things. The bad thing about commission is that it can build a false sense of security. This makes discussing performance difficult because she saw her earnings as evidence that she knew her job pretty darn well. Her arrogance at our first performance meeting was disturbing to me, her boss and our Human Resource Manager. She knew that she made more money than us and she equated that with being superior. We were wasting her time. She changed her tune drastically six months later when her customer announced their move to China. In that meeting she was begging us to not cut her pay as abruptly as her customer had stopped buying from us. I told her that I would give her one week extension of pay for every minute that she was in the negotiations that lead to opening this account. She sure proudly strutted her stuff when she cashed her commission checks, but the truth is she had no part of the negotiations to close that business, but she reaped the commission from it for three years. Debbie truly did a good job helping us serve the customer, but she had nothing to do with acquiring the business in the first place. It is easier to cook and serve than it is to catch the fish. Debbie was regularly attending seminars to improve her performance, but she didn't apply her knowledge. She wasn't wise. Worse, she was arrogant. It was her boss and I that afforded her the opportunity in the first place. Her first two years in sales, she sucked up everything that we had to say like a sponge. After three years, she thought that she knew it all. She stepped on too many fingers and toes climbing her ladder and now she didn't receive the support that she had in the past. She wasn't able to devote the time that she needed to because her personal life kept interrupting and she got busier trying to hide. We actually discussed putting her back in a marketing role which she thought was insulting. Funny, she was proud to be the Marketing Manager for six years, now it was beneath her.

We saw the writing on the wall with her number one bread & butter account and we warned her to take the marketing position or, if the rumors were true, and they were closing their operations in the states, her pay would drop from $113,140/year from the prior year to $12,300/year with commission from the remaining customers that she served. She said she couldn't afford to and that she would hang in there. This she did for another year and then the customer moved to Mexico, as rumored and her job was eliminated. All she had to do was 40 hours of work each week doing the basics that she knew and stretch a little at learning to close new business. Her boss was willing to teach her and happy to help her close. But Debbie wouldn't follow. She was too proud to accept her old job back and go to work for $52,000/year. She opted for unemployment benefits and I have no idea how long she didn't work. At the height of her career she earned $178,000. Today she is an office manager making less than $40,000 a year. No manicures for her anymore. She blames this on the migration of work to Mexico, but in truth, she is totally responsible for the loss. Debbie lost her job because she stopped working, she stopped following direction and she was spiritually bankrupt.

Debbie never missed church when she was a single mother struggling to make it on her manager's salary. She began taking golf lessons on Sundays to fit into the sales role better. She made a Sunday golf game a part of her new lifestyle and she joined the country club. Debbie was such an eager learner during her first few years in the organization. But once her income level sky-rocketed, she became arrogant and lost most of her friends. She would say she changed friends. What she changed was her relationship to her God, and He changed the rest.

Judith Bardwick wrote a wonderful book called "Danger in the Comfort Zone". This book talks candidly about the entitlement mentality (people who show up for work and think that's enough), its affects on our business world and what can be done about it. She goes into detail about how people work and how stress factors affect performance. She talks about the many contributing factors that create the Debbies and Freds of the world. I absolutely agree with her. I have heard her speak and she is spot on. What I am adding that she hasn't is the spiritual consequences of entitlement, for the individual, the organization and society that we live in. She hasn't identified it as a spiritual problem and I am saying it is absolutely a spiritual problem and the solution is absolutely a spiritual remedy.

"In all labor there is profit" Proverbs 14:23. "A rebuke goes deeper into one who has understanding than a hundred blows to a fool" Proverbs 17:10. "Do not weary yourself to gain wealth. Cease from your consideration of it. When you set your eyes on it, it is gone. For wealth certainly makes itself wing; like an eagle that flies towards the heavens." Proverbs 23: 4-6. "He who restrains his words has knowledge, and he who has a cool spirit is a man of understanding. Even a fool, when he keeps silent, is considered wise." Proverbs 17:27&28. These proverbs are keys to the spiritual answers that we need to have going on here.

We need to value labor appropriately. In all labor there is profit. Working gets reward. If we expect to grow we need to take risks. When that doesn't work out there may be some form of rebuke, when we screw up at work there may be some form of rebuke. When we learn a new trade we will make mistakes. Sometimes we will fail. Failure can be depressing as an individual and devastating to an organization. We often do not see the opportunities that failure can open up. "In truth, it's usually failure, disappointment, and frustration that motivates people to reexamine that which they've taken for granted. It's rare to find a big change without significant bad news. It's only when the old ways of doing things are clearly not working that the path is cleared for new ways to be introduced. After all, if the old ways continue to generate success, it's immensely difficult to argue successfully for change. In that sense, the pain of failure creates the largest opportunities for progress.

When times are scary, it's hard to feel optimistic. Big changes are usually frightening. But in the long run, stepping up to change and dealing with it usually has positive outcomes. The written Chinese word for crisis consists of two symbols: one meaning hard times and the other opportunity." (Bardwick, 229)

I graduated in 1977 from Bowdoin. I landed my first corporate job that summer working for a wonderful company named Grede Foundries. I had to move from New England to Milwaukee Wisconsin. I left my parents home in Connecticut and my father Herb shook my hand and looked me in the eye and said, "I know you just graduated from Bowdoin, but nobody wants to hear anything you have to say. Keep your mouth shut and listen." I drove for 7 hours and stopped and met my paternal grandfather on the New York State Thruway. I called him Holysmokes. We ate lunch and he handed me $100 and said, "Do yourself a favor, for your first year keep your mouth shut and listen." I thanked Holysmokes and continued my drive to my maternal grandparents who lived on Grand Island, New York for the night; I stayed with Glick & Granny. Glick taught me more about work and horses than any other man as I grew up. He was a union electrician; he was the first man hired and the last let go on the Niagara Power Project. I gained my love for horses from him, my bald head and my Scots-Irish revolutionary propensity. As I left a tearful granny and a proud Glick, he said to me; "just remember you will meet the same people on your way up the ladder that you will see on your way down and keep your mouth shut and listen." I don't have a grandson, so America KEEP YOUR MOUTH SHUT AND LISTEN! Know your rank and be thankful to be alive at this time of man. Never stop being a student, never lose your edge and respect your elders and superiors!

Solomon talks about not focusing on money, I know he gave us the proverbs about the ant, locust, badger, lizard and lion because he wants us to focus on these attributes and serve God and man with our special talents, then God promises to provide for us. "It is by his deeds that a lad distinguishes himself if his conduct is pure and right. The hearing ear and the seeing eyes, the Lord has made both of them. Do not, love sleep lest you become poor; open your eyes, and you will be satisfied with food." Proverbs 20:11-13. My father and grandfathers were trying to tell me the same thing!

Strip away all of the trapping of your job and look at what you do. Does it really contribute to profit? If you took 3 months off work, could your business survive? Not would your projects get done, would there be a profit? If profit goes on when you're gone, then are you really needed? Wake up and smell the tea! XYZ Corporation doesn't care about you, God does. He measures your work and rewards you accordingly, always. Like the mother fox, some days you'll miss the squirrel, other days a big rabbit will cross your path. But if you're not out hunting you won't get either. Keep hunting! Go to work each day like it's your first day on the job! If you are not employed, God still expects an eight hour day from you. I'm talking about working, not employment. Put all of your Transactions before God and listen and he will communicate what He wants you to do. I know too much sleep isn't on the list.

When we look at the productivity of our society the standard bell curve exists. At one end are the slugs we need to step on. Besides them moving up the curve are the locusts and ants that need to be retrained and their performance improved. Further up the curve we find the average worker. The performance and contribution increase as we slide down the other side of the bell curve where the stars and super stars live. Our problem of followership rests on the left side of the curve, but leadership impacts both sides of the curve. It is the leaders fault if you have a super star doing non value added work. We have two separate but related issues; the slugs who don't work enough and those ants who work hard doing nothing of value. One significant difference between the two is that God WILL, provide for the latter over time, and he will punish the slugs throughout his or her life with unsavory consequences for their lack of effort. Unfortunately, both the ant and the slug may face the same immediate consequence when a business fails, but over time, the ant will be back on his feet and the slug will be sleeping, watching television and wondering why he isn't finding work.

The way to begin to change anything significant about ourselves is through prayer. There are many different components to prayer. The serenity prayer can be a great place to start. We ask for courage to change the things we can, and wisdom to understand the things that we can't change. What we can most easily change is our own attitude. Everything else takes more work. Dr. Creflo Dollar says that those who live in the spirit will keep so busy doing God's work they won't be able to indulge in sin. He says we cannot will this into place, but we can pray this into place. Our mind set has to change to really believe that if an action doesn't align with the word, it is wrong. There is no right way to do the wrong thing. One who thinks this way cannot justify being a slug no matter how horrible our boss or working conditions are. Because there is nothing in the word that says being a slug is all right. If your company is going out of business and you are still collecting a wage, God expects that you will still exchange work for money. No matter how juicy the gossip is, there is nothing in the word that says it is right to gossip. In fact it says the opposite, it is wrong to gossip. If it doesn't align with the word, don't do it! This has nothing to do with company policy or rules. In fact I'll guarantee that if you live and work in alignment with the word, then you won't even need to know the company rules to live within them. God's standards are higher than the world's.

Changing an addiction or bad habit can be a horrible experience. Bad work habits are habits none the less. I'm hoping to begin a "Slug & Gossip" rehab business after this book is written. Why? To improve the quality of their lives so they can become productive contributing members of our society. No kidding the same processes may be needed to change the habits of work that are used to address addictions of other types. Personally I prefer firing them and hiring people whose potential and performance reflect one another. But this isn't compassionate and doesn't align with the word so this is a wrong action initially. So for now we need to awaken America to the truth about the danger to all of our lives that bad work habits bring our national economy and security. We need to address this with the same fervor that we have attacked racism during the last four decades. The change is significant. It has taken a lot of trial and error, this will too. It starts with zero tolerance stuff, at home!

How we work is very important to God. If we are His children then we will show this in how we perform everything; appearance, fitness, humility, eager to learn, excited to produce and happy to accommodate. We will also show it in how we value time, peace, love and commitment.

We will show it in how we value time when we take advantage of every second by performing our work like a concert pianist, every time we flip that burger, write that report, and talk with an employee or customer. If you can say; "I've been doing it that way for years!" then I suggest that there may have not been any improvement, or innovation and either "it" will be becoming obsolete soon or you will! God has no expiration date, He is never obsolete. Practices become obsolete as soon as better practices are developed. Principles are set in place, they don't develop. Jesus gave a parable more than once about talents or money. He talked of a master who had 3 slaves and gave one of them 10 talents, one of them 5 talents and the last one 1 talent, then he went on a journey. The first 2 slaves invested the money and proudly gave the master his money back plus the money they earned. The last slave buried the talent for safety, but when he gave it back to the master he blamed the master in saying that he knew his master was a harsh man so he didn't want to risk losing the only talent that he was given so he simply buried the money. The master took the talent from him and gave to the man with the most talents. Jesus goes on to say that to those who have abundance, more will be given and to those who have little, even that will be taken away. Then Jesus said the master cast the slave into darkness, even though the slave gave him back his talent. This is clear that God wants us to give Him back more than the talents he gives us initially by taking risks, working hard, being innovative, creative and loyal. But above all the last slave wasn't a lizard, he did nothing, he was a slug! He had time to do work and wasted it; he didn't value it or spend it.

We show how we value peace by being peaceful. This we demonstrate when we don't contribute to unrest, gossip or conflict. How we handle differences and crises shows our own character to our entire work world every day. Are we part of the problem or are we always working on solutions? Do we value our way or the way that best fits the needs of the organization? Do we seek to be understood first or to understand?

We demonstrate that we value love by how we treat our fellow man, woman and child. This shouldn't vary from

115

person to person because of rank. Earlier I talked about looking at each person like they were your mother. I adore my mother. I happily accommodate her and I try to make sure she feels secure. Being trustworthy in your relationships is a great indicator of valuing love.

God looks with a watchful eye at our commitment. Covenants mean a great deal to God and man. When we take a job we agree to exchange time and energy for money. We make covenants as we are filling out the W-2's and sign off that we've read the company hand book. In God's eyes these are as sacred as a marriage license. When we hire anybody we expect that we are exchanging the wage we agree to for their best efforts at everything, every day. Nobody wants to pay for mediocrity or worse.

 People that are good workers always resent those who don't pull their weight. But instead of talking to the slugs, we talk about them and nothing changes. Jesus tells a great parable about a man who owned a vineyard who hires workers throughout the day and agrees to pay them the same daily wage regardless of what time of the day he hired them. Naturally, the people who worked all day resented those that were hired later in the day but received the same wage. I said naturally because this is our nature. The owner of the vineyard rebukes the angry workers because it is his vineyard, his money and none of their business what he chooses to pay each person.

He made a commitment with each individual. As long as he honored his commitment God blessed the transaction regardless of the level of pay and the fairness that the men naturally perceived. Much of the time being a child of God requires us to fight our nature, this is one of them. I have never seen anything in the Bible that says there is a guarantee of fairness anywhere. But much is written on how to respond to being treated unfairly. Loyalty means we honor our commitment in spite of difficulties and unfairness. Jesus used this parable to illustrate the possibility of an equal Heaven for sinners regardless at which point in their lives they accepted God. The two points that I want to raise are that people are motivated one way or another by a relationship between how much work they do, versus how much work their peers do. They always compare that to how much each person gets paid. The other point is that the man who owns the vineyard sets the rules and determines how he distributes his assets. This balance is critical to creating an environment that succeeds for the owner, the skilled and the unskilled. Most of our corporate workplaces conform to standards for distributing the resources of the business to its employees based on job classification, market value of the positions, and longevity with the company. Frankly I think that we do a pretty good job of it overall today in America. The commitments that companies make to its associates today are the fairest, clearest and most closely scrutinized in history. Why aren't we motivated to do our best as a result? Because we don't step on the slugs that kill morale and we focus on practices at work instead of principles.

There is the old joke about doctors and lawyers always practicing their job so they call it a practice. In truth all of our jobs are practices. Athletics, music, the arts, acting all requires hours and hours of practice to succeed. When we hear somebody brag of working someplace doing something for 30 years we are expected to equate a high level of expertise in that person's job. Thirty years everyday represents a lifetime of practice. Looking back over 30 years the changes to our world are staggering. These changes directly impact all of us and the practices that we use every day. But the principles reflecting how we should behave toward one another don't change. Basic behavioral habits that demonstrate honesty, integrity, industrious work ethic, understanding of rank and role versus position and tasks, will yield a far greater return over time than will becoming an expert in any specific tasks. I became an expert in film manufacturing. Thirty years ago this would be a highly marketable set of skills to have. Today there is no film industry and what's left has more expertise available than I could ever compete with. However, the leadership habits that I have developed from 35 years in the manufacturing management world are highly transferable regardless of the product being manufactured or the technologies used in the manufacturing process.

Stephen Covey wrote the 7 Habits of Highly Effective People, Deepak Chopra wrote the 7 Spiritual Laws of Success. If one combines the two books one touches on 14 principles that if practiced daily will develop habits that can enable one to create a life of meaningful contribution and abundance. I am not trying to re-invent their wheels; I'm trying to get their wheels turning. I could come up with 7 Laws of work that will guarantee you a lifetime spiritual career, but God included everything that you need to know in His works. James emphasizes in Chapter 2:24 "You see that a man is justified by works, and not by faith alone." We are all important to God. He wants to see our works every day. If you have a job; do it better each day, be a cheerful, positive role model each day, try to learn something new every day. Be your own toughest critic, the tougher you are on yourself, the easier your boss will be. Always go the extra mile for the customer, your boss and your coworkers.

The weekend of the 4th of July is very busy at the ranch and we had a "walk along" scheduled around 3:00pm. Typically this means, putting a small child on one of our most bomb-proof horses and leading them around a small corral 4 times. When the family arrived for their walk along, this boy had a cousin with him. There were 3 adults and 2 small boys from Indonesia. With some guidance, I let the boys pick out their horses and I took the entire group for a walk along the trail in the shade. It was over 90 degrees and I had been working since daybreak, but the experience that the entire group had walking together on a beautiful trail instead of 4 circles in a dusty, hot pen was exhilarating for everybody and before the family left they signed up to do it again the next day. When the waitresses at the ranch serve our young children guests their dinner, this also includes cutting their meat. We all try diligently to go the extra mile for all of our guests and we get a great deal of repeat business! We all proudly exude a rancher's work ethic. We also eagerly fill in the gaps that get created by the ever changing dynamics of the business. We don't sit by and watch the gaps get bigger and do nothing because "it's not my job". It may be these gaps that grow into new jobs!

If you don't have a job; get up and work when the sun rises! There is an old story of a young man who finds a beautiful horse. He runs home with the horse and shows his father and says; "isn't it wonderful to find this beautiful horse?" to which his father replied; "maybe yes, maybe no." The next day the young man saddles his new horse and tries to ride it. The horse bucks and kicks and the young man falls off and breaks his leg. When he returns home badly injured he says to his father; "isn't it horrible that I have broken my leg and cannot work?" to which his father replied; "maybe yes, maybe no." The next day his country declares war on its neighboring country and all young men are drafted into service. Two weeks later the men from this young man's home town are all killed in battle. The moral to the story is that we never know when something is a good thing or a bad thing when the Universe is helping you grow. If a broken leg becomes a blessing, so can unemployment. In fact to those whose previous job was out of sync with one's God given talents, this could be the greatest blessing of your life! You truly have an opportunity to re-create yourself. The word recreation means to take a break from work to recharge, re-direct and re-commit. But the Universe wants you to get up, turn off the television and go to work.

There are 3 types of following; blind followership, bland followership and believing followership. There are times when we need to be a blind follower. When we begin a new job or assignment it is essential that one do what one is told by our new boss. Always seek first to understand. Usually the only way to really understand something is to experience it and feel the consequences of different choices. The blind man needs assistance and guidance to move about, so will blind followers. There are many times that we hire people who have limited intelligence or language skills to do tasks that require little education. Or we hire somebody who is a weak person who will do what you say always. These people need work and we need them. This requires a higher level of supervision and inspection of work. The total costs to your business for having a low skill level work force may exceed what your labor cost could be if you hire a higher caliber of person, paid more and had no supervision. The hidden costs of low skill include; a higher absentee level, longer learning curves, lower quality and productivity, limited transferability of skills, higher turnover and low promote-ability of existing members of your workforce. You get what you pay for. If you want blind followers, then be a diligent supervisor and watch their work! We need blind followers, pay them respectably.

We may need to be blind followers even if we supervise others. When a new company policy or practice is being implemented and it is our responsibility to educate our workforce about the new policy and enforce this change whether we believe it is the best thing or not, it is imperative that you introduce this policy with conviction and faith that it is the right thing to do at this time. When we present these kinds of changes as something you don't believe in, your team will not consider it important and implementation of this change will be lackluster at best. But worse, your team will see that you don't totally support your superior's leadership and direction. Why should they? If you don't follow well, your team won't honor followership. When a decision has been reached from above and your direction is to execute the plan, then damn the torpedoes and full speed ahead. Be the blind follower your boss needs.

The real problem is the bland follower. Unfortunately, this represents the bulk of our adult workforce. These people comply; these people do what they perceive that they are paid to do. They have really never lived as a winner; they are the lambs, not the lions. The lamb never really stands out and his end is getting his hair repeatedly removed, then when he gets plump, he gets eaten.

A real manager lives a steady stream of benefit cost analysis. They know in their mind each moment what the budgets that they are responsible for are and how they stand against them. They know how their choices impact profit and they act to maximize profit, safety and trust at all times. They act and initiate action. But above all they are teachers to the people they supervise.

They're emotionally solid and have high levels of energy. People seek them out for direction. If that isn't you, then you shouldn't be a manager or a leader. You should learn to follow well. Shame on companies who put people in these positions who are not great teachers or who are not ethical standouts. Truly I say to you that you'd be better off with a few great communicating leaders and a great force of followers than a staff of expensive, bland leaders. Actually that's an oxymoron! One cannot be a true leader and be bland. The position of Bland is reserved for managers. Real leaders are never bland. But the US workforce is full of bland middle managers, engineers, sales people and maintenance workers. When you are truly tied into the dynamics of a business there are no start times and quitting times, astute managers and leaders who respond to the ever changing demands of a going concern need to be as prepared as firefighters.

When leaders don't lead, what's a follower to do? In our case they usually spend time talking about the lack of leadership in the company and use this for justification of their own mediocrity. They take ownership in their tasks and lose all sight, if they ever had it, about why they work. There are a number of signs that I read in offices that people think are cute. One reads; "Lack of planning on your part, does not constitute an emergency on my part". I say that if the emergency is a threat to safety, profitability or work environment, then it shouldn't matter whose poor planning caused the issue. What this sign says is; "I'm not going to hustle! I don't understand why I'm here."

I look at the hours of a typical business and when I have salaried managers who get there 5 minutes before start time and end their day at quitting time day in and day out, I know that they're not creating anything for the business, they're maintaining tasks. They may work hard, they may be wonderful employees, but do they earn their pay? If you are more concerned with doing your tasks (practices) well than you are about company profit, ROI and new customer development, (principles), then your mindset needs adjustment. If you go to work each day to do your job instead of to improve your own performance, then you are courting obsolescence. You need to understand how quickly the life cycles of products and services expire in today's dynamic market place and that this translates to how quickly your services may or may not be needed.

Most importantly if you think that your company owes you anything beyond your promised pay and benefits, you are WRONG! We are paid for services rendered for a time period. Rarely are we paid today for exemplary performance done 8 years ago. But many people feel that the company owes them for some great contribution done at some long ago time. The truth is our pay check usually reflects a period of time worked. Once one cashes the check, the company and you are even. The fox that survives never stops hunting. It doesn't matter how old the fox gets. There are no young foxes that are going to hunt for their mother 3 years from now when she gets too old. My father worked for the same major steel manufacturer for over 45 years, he sold pig iron, not the lucrative commodity it was in the 50's. They don't need much pig iron today and don't make much of it in this country. His company doesn't exist anymore and my mother's pension is less than $130 a month! That's what you get for trusting Company XYZ for 45 years.

To hold on to mindsets that create negative mind chatter will retard your own growth. Thinking about how you are getting short changed instead of concentrating on how you can improve yourself is professionally and spiritually suicidal. It will keep you from becoming the follower that you need to be. Stephen Covey's 1st habit of effectiveness is to be pro-active. This begins by taking total responsibility for your performance, your circumstances, your health, your life and your contribution. When your mind chatter wallows in resentment and blame, it makes it very difficult to turn your circumstances around. You will stay bland.

The greatest problem isn't the lack of productivity that we may experience. It is the increase in negative mind energy that pollutes our universe. The universe provides abundantly and doesn't like to be dismissed. The old television commercial for some butter substitute used to tout that it isn't nice to fool Mother Nature. When we don't realize our true potential and we waste the precious time we are blessed with to live up to the glorious potential God had planned for us to contribute with, we will experience loss and scarcity. This exacerbates the problems of negative mind chatter, gossip and sloth. This dangerous vicious cycle fills the universe with more negative energy which manifests itself in more unemployment, hurricanes, earthquakes, volcanoes, oil wells run amuck and war. Am I saying that screwing off at work can lead to war? Yes! But that's a topic for another book.

Is it possible to go from bland to something more? Absolutely! Immediately! For anybody who has tried to quit smoking, lose weight or begin an exercise program, change isn't easy although it is usually simple…."just do it" is easier said than done. Most change requires support and guidance. Hey, that's God, your boss and your conscience.

Most of the time what is needed most to improve from bland to better, begins with reparation or re-definition of relationships. This begins with an honest personal assessment. In AA's 12 step program they call it a personal inventory. There are three questions one needs to answer; what am I doing today and is what I'm doing necessary and done well? Believe it or not, engineers tend to be great at studying, figuring and setting standards, although they may be able to do advanced calculus, they have trouble doing math. The kind of math I'm talking about is basic business sense. Sales people tend to be great coming out of the gate, but do they finish the race? Do they win? Only a few do. Why? Middle managers tend to have been great workers, maybe great supervisors. What happens to keep them from working once they get an office? One answer to all of these questions is followership. We humans get to be 35 and we think we have it figured out. We have kids, homes, responsibilities and we don't like to be challenged by another human or criticized or told our effort isn't good enough. We respond like teenagers when we are confronted by our boss, if our boss has the cojones to confront us... most don't.

We come home from work and we want the world to look at us as competent. Can you look in the mirror and really say that you are the best in the world at what you do? Or was there something at work today that you could have done better, or more of? If you don't ask these questions of yourself, you're a chump, not a champ. Then you need to humble yourselves and understand your rank and role. I recommend that you undertake the same kind of work sampling on your daily activities that I described earlier on and see for yourself how you spend your time. Once you have a brutally honest assessment of your activities, then look deeply at each activity and study your practices for improvement. Once you have a clear understanding of what you do during your day, you need to do a study of your personal bank accounts with your coworkers.

Stephen Covey has a concept he calls emotional bank accounts. He says that trust can only be realized if we have positive emotional bank account balances with those we interact with. There are actions that we do that build trust and then there are those that destroy trust. When we break trust we make a withdrawal from the emotional bank account. When our actions build trust, we make a deposit. The problem with trust is that it takes time to build, but it rarely erodes over time, it gets destroyed. In fact it takes many deposits before we can even our balance from a single withdrawal. This is why our actions and words are so important. The time and energy that it takes to build trust can be obliterated with a stupid word or an action that compromises your integrity, in an instant. It is impossible to really trust a gossip because one knows that as soon as you leave the room, you become the next topic of conversation.

"If I make deposits into an Emotional Bank Account with you through courtesy, kindness, honesty, and keeping my commitments to you, I build up a reserve. Your trust toward me becomes higher, and I can call upon that trust many times if I need to. I can even make mistakes and that trust level and Emotional Bank Account reserve, will compensate for it. My communication may not be clear, but you'll get my meaning anyway. You won't make me "an offender for a word." When the trust account is high, communication is easy, instant, and effective."

"But if I have a habit of showing discourtesy, disrespect, cutting you off, overreacting, ignoring you, becoming arbitrary, betraying your trust, threatening you, or playing little tin god in your life, eventually my Emotional Bank Account is overdrawn. The trust level gets very low." (Covey, 188)

Remember our goal is to be effective and we need to be trustworthy to effectively motivate others. It is our job to be effective workers. It is our responsibility to have honorable working relationships with our coworkers, as adults. Our responsibility, not their responsibility! As a good follower we can only control our own actions, words and thoughts. We can impact others' words, thoughts and actions by our own words and actions, but we cannot control others. As an effective leader/manager, it is your job to set your followers up for success by assigning them value added work, clearly defined, closely monitored and fairly compensated for. It is also your job to create an environment where people feel respected and secure. If you can actually create a workplace that is fun and success is celebrated, then you will have a great career as a leader.

I have several friends who tell me that the people who really need this book wouldn't be the kind of people who buy this kind of book. I have to agree. When I look at the people as individuals who I have known that represent this kind of poor followership, they don't read. They don't see themselves as not working. They fought two and a half hours of traffic to get to work 15 minutes early and they were there all day. How dare I say they don't work! Let me tell you about Joe.

Joe the Accounting Manager is 52 years old and has been in the widget business and this firm his whole life. He's done it all. Like most manufacturing firms, Joe's business operated on monthly income statements that needed to be complete 3 working days after close of the month. He had a staff of 6 to handle all accounting functions; payroll, accounts payables, accounts receivables, collections, costing and systems. This team of people worked like animals from the day before the period closed, until the send button was pushed, forwarding the financials to corporate, this usually took 4-5 days.

The remainder of the month this team of people settled down into a routine of tasks and banter. Joe did nothing but gossip, attend meetings, play computer games and check out match.com. In fact Joe loves the computer so much that he actually goes to the office every day for hours and uses the computer for his own use. But he's at the plant so he credits it with working. Actually Joe never misses a chance to let the people at corporate know that he "worked" all weekend, by sharing weekend plant gossip with anyone who would answer their phone on Monday. Joe made $98,000 a year. The Accounting Lead, Megan did all of the day-to-day management of the department as Joe bragged about what a delegator he was. Megan was 28 years old and made $32,400 a year and was a single mom of two. If she missed a week of work, things went to hell. If Joe missed a week of work, nobody would notice.

Joe was a great follower on many levels. But he wasn't a leader of any kind. In fact he was a flirt and a dork, what an attractive combination. He wasn't taken seriously and his position truly wasn't needed. In fact the department was over staffed by 2 not including Joe, compared to most of the plants in the corporation of similar size. But Joe closed the books accurately, on time, every month, so he was never a concern to his boss or corporate. He did his job, he worked every weekend! When I was challenged to submit a budget that was 28% lower than our current year's budget, I suggested that we let Joe go. Corporate accounting called me with our corporate human resources manager on the phone and my boss, the division VP then I was raked over the coals for even suggesting that we let a life-long employee, like Joe, go. Even though Joe's office was next to mine and my boss never set foot in our office, I was told that I had no idea what a great contribution Joe made each day. They just didn't want a lawsuit.

Our plant was sold to a competitor 4 months later mostly because it wasn't as profitable as it should have been. I was transferred to another division. The new company did a cost review and found that the accounting office could function with 4 people. Joe was let go, so was Megan and another great worker named Leslie. The new company didn't value Joe's length of service; in fact it was considered a handicap. Joe would have to learn a whole new system and he was way over paid, as most long term employees are. The new outfit transferred an up and coming cost accountant from their corporate office to replace Joe at $60,000 a year. This was a big raise and promotion for him. The new company did the right thing. Joe's lack of management and leadership was one of the many reasons that the costs of running that plant were out of control and that they were sold! His poor performance cost hard working followers like Megan and Leslie their jobs.

What could have been done differently? Joe was a perfect example of owning practices and not principles. Joe accurately delivered the company profit picture each month without regard to the meaning of lower profits.

He forecasted his demise each week with numbers that he never interpreted to mean a threat to his job. He felt secure because he did his tasks well and secure because he had seniority. Even though the information he delivered to everybody told him that his own costs were out of control and as a result, his job along with everybody's job was in jeopardy.

Had Joe been a good manager/leader he would have replaced his personal computer time with tasks that could have easily eliminated the need for one of his staff. He would have worked within the organization to see where his valuable workers could contribute by doing other tasks that were needed. Megan would have been a perfect fit for a position that was available in the Quality Assurance department. Leslie was a candidate for an opening in production. Neither got the opportunity with the new company because the new management team went after positions without regard to whether they were stepping on ants or slugs. Joe could have improved his systems to minimize the need for redundancies in his departments, instead of spending his time fueling the gossip mill. Had Joe done his job as an engaged manager who took ownership of the actual cost performance of the business unit (principles) and not just keeping score (practices), his department would have easily identified costs problems that our manufacturing team could have fixed.

The truth is had I been allowed to get rid of the dead wood middle managers as I proposed, the company would have far exceeded the profit requirements needed to not be considered a salable entity. The new company bought this business because they saw the potential profit picture if they simply followed sound business basics. The new company ended up getting rid of every manager that was on my hit list. The original owner didn't want to get rid of any of the middle managers because they were afraid to have any legal actions against them undertaken while they were going through the due diligence process for the sale of the business. They didn't really care about these employees; they just didn't want their plans disturbed. In the end everybody at that business unit lost because the new company bought the business strategically to serve their overall end which meant eventually moving the business to their facility being built in China in two years. There is no plant today and 178 Americans lost their jobs to a group of better followers who are paid slave wages and work in hell holes! Had the business unit performed to its potential all along, I know it would still be here in America with more employees than it supported before. Today Megan and Leslie have great jobs. They got these jobs because they went after them and they had great references. You can't keep a good ant down.

Joe is working for a seasonal tax preparation firm for less than $20,000 a year which is about what he was worth all along. He is miserable and does nothing but complain about how unfairly he was treated. He wallows in this negative mind chatter. He will die there. Make no mistake about it, Joe's performance along with the performance of 3 of his co managers cost 178 people their jobs. All four of these managers thought that they worked hard.

We are losing to better followers than us and the crime is that our great American superstar corporations recognize this and go where it is easier and less expensive to lead and manage. Why pay $15 an hour for somebody who questions authority and wants $16 /hour to do mediocre work, when you can pay $16 a week for an employee who is pleased to have an opportunity to do what you tell them to because they were raised that way. The added profit contributions made by not requiring pollution controls, safety equipment or not paying extra benefits at all is even greater encouragement to transfer jobs. We Americans are being out worked! This has never changed throughout all of history. When man is motivated, there really is very little that we cannot accomplish collectively. When man gets fat, comfortable and lazy, he gets knocked out, whether you are talking about the Roman Empire or Tiger Woods who just lost the British Open to who from South Africa? Be a lean, mean, fighting machine whether you are a person or a nation.

Both wage rates need to be examined. Is $15/hour really getting you $15/hour of value? If you had a business and hired a friend to work for you, would you only pay him $16/week, if he worked hard all week? I think that if we had slaves, most of us would treat them better than manual laborers live in China. If you would strike against your company for more wages or benefits, how can you justify buying products from companies who pay their workers worse than slaves? I don't think that if most Americans had to work for minimum wage and work extremely hard all day, that they would display a joyful countenance. On the other hand, many people world-wide, would be walking on clouds to have that exact job. The $7.50/hour would be extravagant. What we over pay some people who work doing jobs that could easily be done by the average chimpanzee is disgusting with some of our old established unionized corporations.

We used to be tough, that's how we became America! We can be that tough again and we desperately need to do that today. Things won't get better until each one of us get better. Better countenance breeds better countenance. Accomplishing something feels good. Helping others feels great. Doing anything well feeds pleased countenance. Forget about the money, think about countenance management. One may argue that when you are unemployed, looking for work and have a family to feed and a mortgage to pay, that genuinely exuding a pleased countenance is a tall order, and may not be possible. I say; accomplish something, help someone and do everything you do, well. Be thankful that you have a family. Then see how that affects your countenance. If that doesn't make a positive change, I'd be surprised. Then do a little more tomorrow and a little more the day after that and so on. If you are employed and you are a slug or a gossip, then you had better rethink your life. As Creflo Dollar always says you need to change your "mind-set". If you are a boss and you employ slugs or gossips, then you need to make changing those people's work habits, a priority. If that cannot be done, you need to fire them. Then we as a society need to not extend to them unemployment benefits like we do for other causes for termination. We need to honor all work and dishonor all sloth at all levels, at home, in schools and in our communities. I am in favor of extending unemployment benefits to everyone who is then required to work for the communities that they live in. They should also submit the volunteer activities they've participated in and the classes they took while they received benefits for the last year. To pay people to sit home and watch television and take extra naps isn't solving anything.

There is plenty to do in our nation. There is never a day where Someplace, USA hasn't had a natural or man-made disaster. Fill the New York shores with our unemployment benefit recipients. House them in tents and feed them gruel and water, but put them to work cleaning up the mess from hurricane Sandy. In the history of man we live extremely high on the hog, even our unemployed have a great quality of life compared to the rest of humanity. Way too high! Our expectations of fairness, comfort, healthcare, home ownership are way out of line with the rest of humanity and life on this planet.

We need to be careful about taking too much emotional ownership in the tasks that we get paid for. Do them well, but always look at tasks as something that will soon become, obsolete. The principle of doing tasks well will not become obsolete. We should become as adroit at learning new jobs and finding a new job as we become at any tasks we are assigned once we are employed. We have to look at periods of scarcity or unemployment as normal and as a golden opportunity to change for the better. We need to understand the fundamental business principles that enable the growth of jobs. Business is war, it is not fair. Why should we expect fair from a mathematical entity. To hold mindsets that build expectations that are unrealistic is asking for failure. Expectations are resentments under construction. Resentment is a prime motivation killer and it is truly one of the only things that we as individuals can actually control. Work on what you can control and pray about those things that you cannot control. Work on your countenance as a number one priority. Have a good day, every day! Seek wisdom and approval from God, and the universe will provide in accordance to your skills and effort. If you want more, become more. Never stop being an ant. God never said that we were to stop schooling ourselves at a certain age. Understand that this is totally each individual's responsibility, not the US Government or XYZ Corporation. If the fox stops hunting, it should starve and die.

I look at this picture of my grandfather Vic Mc Bride in 1939 in Bolivar, New York. He owned a filling station/café/bar. He had a 4 year old daughter, my mom and he and Granny lived on several dollars a day. He eagerly ran from behind the bar as he took off his apron, to happily fill your automobile with gasoline. He washed your windshield, checked your oil and actually saluted his customer while he donned a bow tie. He hustled politely, because he was an American man and that is what he was supposed to do. He had no health insurance, his first wife and child died during childbirth. He didn't get his first pair of shoes until he was twelve. He had to have shoes to go to work. I began work in earnest at thirteen as did my sister Cindy. We worked on a farm. I picked vegetables in the hot sun all day while she worked up front selling them. There are still a lot of American kids on farms and ranches that work hard all summer long. My father and grandfather conditioned me from birth that work was a major part of being a man. We didn't have to work, we were allowed to work. My father expected that I would work at age 13, but truthfully, I wanted very much to work and earn my own money. My parents made becoming a teenager a major stepping stone, it was a source of pride to work like an adult, because we were becoming adults. I have paid my own way since then so has my sister, both of us are happy people. We were treated with respect at home for working and we were corrected immediately and corporally for sloth or showing disrespect of any kind to anybody. We were to respect our elders, our superiors and teachers, our country and our President. My father was a Marine so I was raised as a Marine. I loved my father and he was very hard on me by today's standards. Therefore it is possible to hold somebody to extremely high standards, punish harshly when performance or behavior falls short of acceptable and still be loved! I have a friend and he told me how he had to barter with his thirteen year old daughter to get her to clean her room. I have no words printable for this. His daughter has a Thai sister across the globe who has no room and who may be sold into prostitution if her family's small farm doesn't produce and he's going to listen to his daughter talk about fair. We need to condition our young to compete with the Chinese and the Vietnamese, these are tough competitors who eat rodents and sleep 8 to a room.

So we should prepare for what a significant drop in the quality of life here can really mean. It doesn't mean that we cannot find happiness and security. It will mean a redefinition of what the "American Dream" means. Try to think about who should own a home. Imagine only people who can pay cash for their home could own one, the same for cars, boats, college educations. What would your life look like today if you couldn't borrow? That's probably what it should look like. Everything else is a dangerous illusion. In fact the sin on the top ten sin list that we tend to brush off as not significant is coveting. The entire "Keep up with the Jones" thing is coveting in action. In God's eyes it is as serious a sin as murder. But we humans accept it daily every time we allow; "mom, can I have..." We covet and think that this sin doesn't matter. In many cases if we didn't covet, we wouldn't make the choices that separate us from God. We would also be happy with what we had. It would be difficult to go into debt for something one doesn't need. Our debt is killing us and contributes to significant negativity in our collective countenance. We also wouldn't be driven for titles and pay and we could focus on performing our God given gifts to the best of our ability, six days a week for our entire life. If our mind chatter didn't include coveting we wouldn't waste thought on what we imagine our boss has that we don't, we could be a better student to our boss and a better worker for our God. Who do you work for?

Chapter 5

Riding for the brand

COWBOY VALUES

1) Live each day with courage
2) Take pride in your work
3) Always finish what you start
4) Do what has to be done
5) Be tough, but fair
6) When you make a promise, keep it
7) Ride for the brand
8) Talk less and say more
9) Remember that some things are not for sale
10) Know where to draw the line   James P. Owen

Stephen Covey says that we should put first things first. In the Book of Proverbs there is a special chapter devoted to exalting wisdom. Solomon was the wisest King in history. He wrote 3,000 proverbs. The Hebrew term for "proverb" means a comparison. The Book of Proverbs is a library of instruction on cause and effect and how to live life. The theme throughout the book is wisdom for living. In chapter 8 Solomon gives us some fundamental truths about wisdom. The most important tidbits are revealed in verses 22 through 36. This says that wisdom is both older than the universe and fundamental to it. From wisdom flows the joy of creation. Wisdom is what God counted as primary and indispensable. This also warns to heed instruction and be wise. In verses 35 & 36 God says; "For he who finds me (wisdom) finds life and obtains favor from the Lord.

But he who sins against me (wisdom) injures himself."
The Hebrew term for wisdom is "hokmah". This is used
45 times in the Book of Proverbs. The definition of
hokmah is the skill of craftsmen, sailors, singers,
administrators and counselors. Knowledge is the
accumulation of information. Wisdom is the skillful
application of information. To be smart, one learns from
ones mistakes. To be wise one learns from the mistakes
of others. What does it mean to "sin against me"? It
means to not be an ant, locust, badger or lizard and to be
a fool, sloth and gossip. In chapter 8 verses 17 through
22 God says of wisdom; "I love those who love me
(wisdom); and those who seek me will find me, enduring
wealth and righteousness. My fruit is better than gold,
even pure gold, and my yield than choicest silver. I
walk in the way of righteousness in the midst of the path
of justice, to endow those who love me with wealth, that
I may fill their treasuries." He says wisdom brings forth
wealth. He doesn't say all of our life, or all of the time,
but that the exhibition of wisdom throughout one's life
will yield a life of abundance versus a life of scarcity.

So who do you follow? Who are your teachers? Never
before in the history of man is it easier to learn from the
best of the best. One can turn on a computer and go to
YouTube and watch the greatest classical guitarists ever
recorded, or watch great martial arts masters perform, or
take a wild land firefighting course or any number of
classes. We can listen to a sermon from Joel Osteen,
Joyce Meyer or Creflo Dollar any time of any day.
There is no excuse for any American not intentionally
learning something new every day. If we want to be a

society of laws and liberty we need to defend ourselves one way or the other. Wisdom instead of violence seems like the most pleasant alternative. Knowledge isn't power, wisdom is! Take a computer class if that is your need, or attend an automotive mechanics seminar if that is your interest, earn a degree to learn a practice, make sure this is secondary to understanding and applying fundamental principles of life and business, seek that first.

Covey says that we need to sharpen the saw to be effective. For those who haven't read Covey, he is referring to the concept of disciplined study and practice to keep us sharp. He is absolutely correct. The results of a lifetime of saw sharpening with my passions have made my 50's an exciting joy. Last week I gave a small guitar concert along with a performer whom I had never met. Our guitar styles were different but because we have been playing regularly since we were boys, we appeared like we had been playing together for years. It was spontaneous and we created as we fed off one another. A team of people, who have skill in their profession, when inspired, can create beautiful things when they freely apply their talents together.

I have ridden horses for decades and I've had to care for 93 of them as part of my wrangler job. I ride all that can be ridden and those that are learning to be ridden. Each horse is different, but the end result must be the same, we must get from point A to point B and back safely. I stay in the saddle because I have been ejected from the saddle many times, in many ways, some of that was my

143

lack of riding skill. Much of it was because I didn't see it coming. The horse let me have the information but I simply wasn't skillful enough yet to apply it in a timely fashion. Because of those painful experiences, I see it coming today more often than not. The important ingredient for my growth was getting back in the saddle.

Sharpening the saw happens, one tooth at a time. It should be that way with our learning and practice. We need to practice and we need to expand our knowledge daily. This is supposed to be the information age. Hopefully it gives birth to the wisdom age. Reading and meditating on what is read, is a great saw sharpener. This takes only moments a day. Don't try to eat the elephant all at once. Take one small bite at a time and it will be eaten and savored.

The words "kung fu" also relate to skill and wisdom. Literally translated, the words mean "a skill developed over time with the application of energy." There is an old Shaolin saying; "to unlock the mystery of a technique, one must practice it 1,000 times." One can have kung fu at anything that has had time and energy applied to it, the piano, cooking, dance. But one won't have skill without time and energy applied. God gives us our share of time and talent we need to apply the energy. This has absolutely nothing to do with being paid. Again acquiring mastery is a rewarding experience in and of itself. This is a fantastic countenance builder. If you are wise enough to enjoy the journey to mastery, your life will be abundant always. We need to practice kindness and charity. It is work to always be kind. It is a choice to apply energy to the help of others without regard for repayment. But this fills your spiritual bank account and this will spill into your actual bank account.

Before we end each day we should examine our roles and ask if we have become a better God fearing person today, a better family member, friend and employee. We need to analyze our emotional bank account balances. We should also have weekly saw sharpening lists that we rarely neglect. This applies to how much we read, pray, work out or contribute to our family, how often we practice our passions and skills. How many good deeds did we do?

These are actual tasks that can be measured and tallied. If we do these things, we will become better at the roles that we find dear to us and pleasing to God. It is up to us to keep score and always try to beat our best. Don't worry about being the best there is, just try to be the best that we can be. If we behave this way, we will always be afforded opportunity to work for money. Opportunity is created to meet God's needs for our services. But we have to take the ball and run with it from there. If God needs an EMT and we spend our time watching ER on television instead of getting EMT certified, you can be sure God won't afford us an opportunity to get that EMT job even though we have a genuine interest in emergency medicine and may have acquired some useful knowledge.

Our President can say all he wants about extending benefits to non workers who are unemployed. He has to, they elected him. I did not. But I would still lay down my life for the President of the United States if he commanded me to, because that would be answering to a higher authority. If he wants my life, he has but to ask. It is my God-given job to be a patriot and follow the orders of our commander in chief. I believe that the President wouldn't ask me to lay down my life unless America needed me to, then it would be a great honor and blessing to die in battle for God's purpose. Even if his motives were wrong, mine would not be. God loves a courageous warrior or a comeback kid. He hates a lazy, stupid, irresponsible steward of His gifts.

Who are your teachers? If you pick the right teacher, God will pick the right boss when the time is right. There is an old Zen saying; "When the student is ready a teacher will appear." We should rejoice in the fact that we have the technological capability to access great teachers of all things possible. But the student must be ready! That's us. If you allow your boss to be your teacher, you are on the road to great followership. What a joy it is to supervise a willing and eager employee. If you are not employed or self employed and you can't say that you have teachers, get on the internet and find some. I know that it sounds corny, but listen to your heart. Deepak Chopra says that your desires are meant to guide you to your destiny. Learn how to be a master of your passions through participation and practice. Sing the song that God put in your heart and your heart alone.

My ultimate master is Christ. He has provided me with guides to help me be the body part of Christ that He wants me to be. I have studied many Chinese and Japanese Sages, Sun Tzu, Chuang Tzu, Lao Tzu, Yamamoto Tsunetomo and Miyamoto Musashi. I've read the Bible daily for decades now. The Dali Lama is beyond brilliant, he is divinely inspired. I have read the Quran twice. I have even studied L. Ron Hubbard and Scientology. When it comes to fundamental behavioral principles prescribed for good daily living there are very little differences from one sage to another, from one prophet to another. But that only makes sense because principles are universal. Reading the Quran only reinforced my faith in Christ and underscores my respect for our enemy. The Chinese want to compete toe to toe with us economically. The warring Muslim nations want us dead! Either way we are under siege and we don't acknowledge it. I won't tell you what faith to have. I have a Masonic poem by Carl Claudy it reflects how I believe God wants us to view one another's religions.

"The Arabs heard the call for prayer, and the kneeling faithful thronged the square. While on some mountain's lofty height, a dark priest chanted Brahma's might. Amid a monastery's weeds, an old Franciscan counts his beads. While to the synagogue there came a Jew to praise Jehovah's name. The one great God looked down and smiled and counted each his loving child. For Arab, and Brahman, monk and Jew had reached Him through the Gods they knew."

Pick your faith, but live what you pick. There is nothing from any of the sages and prophets or great minds that I have mentioned that supports foolishness, sloth or gossiping. They all tell their followers to do good, honest work. So for the purposes of this book, all roads lead to effective followership. In fact before you unlock the door to any faith you need to follow first. Once you pick your ranch, saddle up and ride for the brand every day.

Vince Lombardi made the Green Bay Packers the greatest football team in the nation while he coached them. His trade mark was extreme discipline and conditioning and he used a simple offense to beat his enemy one play at a time. Vince was a Catholic who went to church every day. He was sure who to follow first. He was a fanatical student of the game of football. He worked extremely hard. Most importantly he loved his players. With that combination he was a great leader who created teams that won and celebrated. But they were the Green Bay Packers, not Vince Lombardi's team. They loved the brand, they were proud to be Packers. They were proud because they won, they won because they worked harder than their competition and the team members were devoted followers. Nobody on the team questioned Vince's authority. There were no doubts as to why he was the boss. Prior to Vince's arrival in Green Bay Wisconsin, the Packers were considered a weak team from Nowhere, USA. They were an embarrassment to play for, one didn't get drafted by Green Bay; you got exiled there.

But winning changes everything and it did for the Green Bay brand. We need to win for our brand as Americans. Too many of us have been losing too long. Winning and losing are habits. This becomes a way of life for people. One may argue that most of us win a few and lose a few. I agree with that. But people usually tend to exhibit propensities one way or another. Typically the difference between the winner and the loser is enthusiasm, tenacity and preparation. All of these items are absolutely under our control. Stephen Covey lists working towards win-win arrangements with people is a habit needed to be effective. The beauty of win-win is that collective countenance improves. With win-lose results the best we can hope for is leaving the collective countenance unchanged. However, we all love a close competition where both parties have prepared and explode with enthusiasm. We constantly pay to watch that. Nobody enjoys watching a blowout victory. We love a close right up to the last minute game. It is extremely sad if you do not get up each day excited to go to work, it is your responsibility to correct this. But until you do, you're always going to be bland.

As our beautiful country grew west and cattle management was a primary industry, the "Brand" became a critical feature as it designated ownership of cattle. More often than not, the configuration of the brand reflected the property and the family that owned it. The brand that I rode under is a heart, representing a love for the land. There is a "J" in the center of the heart for the Jessup family, the owners of the ranch called Sylvan Dale. Back in the old west the brand was the symbol that you worked for or competed with. To the Jessup family, this brand is a part of who they are. This beautiful working guest ranch is on 3,200 acres and was purchased in 1946 by Morris and Tilly Jessup. My boss was their daughter, Susan. She has lived and worked on that ranch her whole life and she is passionate about this business and the people who are employees and guests.

We all work hard, in fact most farmers and ranchers do. We all take pride in being a part of the Sylvan Dale family and we all ride for the brand. If Susan wasn't enthusiastic all of the time, we wouldn't be! Susan hand picks the many employees that help service our guests. People come from all over the world repeatedly to stay at Sylvan Dale, because it is one of the most beautiful places on earth and because they love the way we make their experience special. The people that make up the "we" all exude that American rancher's work ethic. This is a key part of our guest's experience. In fact, many guests bring their children from their suburban homes to work on this ranch, gathering eggs, branding cattle and learning how to be with a horse. They rightfully want their children to understand hard work and where their "Happy Meal" comes from. Everybody who has stayed with us remembers our brand with pleasure.

The first brand that you ride for is your own faith, your God. Be careful to express your faith with your actions more than your words. Strive to have an onlooker become impressed enough to ask; "what is your faith?" because they see God in your behavior. Leave the bumper stickers and T shirts for rock bands and sports teams. After your onlookers ask, the door is open and this is your time to witness with words, but use what is written first, then embellish with your experience. When people see that your faith in Christ yields a countenance that they long for, then you are riding for the brand well. When we are surrounded by people who constantly strive for good, we help ourselves most. Both good and evil are contagious. Joel Osteen has a concept he calls the "Person of Excellence". The best way to represent God is to exude excellence in everything that we do or say. Doing the best right thing we are capable of doing whether anyone is looking or not demonstrates that we believe God is present.

The second brand that you ride for is your family name. The whole trip on this planet is about family. Who you are and what you do has your family brand on it. We all work to support our families and we would defend our families with our life if need be. Everything we say and do effects somebody. Actions + Behaviors = Consequences, always. When our actions and behaviors are noble, productive, have integrity and courage; the consequences will be positive. This adds to the value of our family name. We make each family member stronger with every good deed that we do. We all know what a scandal can do to a family name. I know that all of us would like to see our name in lights somehow during our lifetime. For most of us that won't happen. But if you love God and behave accordingly, you'll see your name in glorious lights when you are welcomed into heaven. Until then we need to trust that what we do matters a whole lot to God's plan.

The third brand we ride for should be the flag for the United States of America. If you don't, get the Bleep out now! We really need patriotism today more than ever before or we need to abandon the concept for our new Chino-American identity and develop patriotism toward that. However one cuts it, patriotism seems right and Godly. We need to love and support our troops. Any American that understands what our troops are living like in the Middle East understands that the contributions that we make here at home in America pale in comparison to the risk and bitter existence our men and women in service are enduring for our freedom. We have our own sons and daughters laying down their lives for our cause, we shouldn't rest until they all come home. During WWII the efforts at home reflected the efforts made by our troops. Remember "Rosy the Riveter"? Either protest the war or support it. That's one of your most precious American rights, but get involved. Stop the war or win it!

The fourth brand that we ride for is our company's logo. Once we make a covenant with a business to serve their purpose, we should wear our company name with pride and understand that once we collect a check, we are an ambassador for this organization at all times. That has responsibilities that far exceed the tasks that may be assigned to you in your particular job. I have found that most people who take a genuine interest and sense of ownership in the businesses that they work for have more fun at work than those who just have a job. It is wise to have fun at work because that is where one spends most of one's waking hours. If you cannot improve the collective countenance at work, why should you be retained as an employee? We need to have a category for employee terminations that reads; didn't make a difference, or contributed to the degradation of the collective countenance, or we just didn't like her. The owner of the vineyard should have absolute say as to who he pays his money to and how much that is. I described the qualities that Hal, Bonnie, Ken, Vic McBride and P.J. McManus displayed throughout their lives. The locust, the ant, the badger, the lizard and the lion, these are the character traits that owners of vineyards are looking for. Fools, sloths, gossips and those that won't ride for the brand need not apply. In fact they should be cast into outer darkness where there is wailing and gnashing of teeth.

The fifth brand that we ride for is the brand that your teachers and schools have given you. When we employ somebody to teach us, we bear their brand and represent their ability as a teacher. There is a saying that there are no bad students, only bad teachers. When you earn a degree, or certificate of achievement or participation, you become more of a person. If you apply what you learned later on, you are wise. This applies to all of your extra activities, the clubs you belong to, the churches, the teams you play on or coach, the music that you play or sing. In everything we do we impact our personal stake holders. For example; if you hit a home run and win the softball game, which wins the championship and your picture is on the front page of the paper, then your church and piano teacher and your Boy Scout troop all take pride in you. Your success makes their collective countenance rise and brings them credibility. If you get caught with child porn, this will hurt membership in your church, you will tarnish the Boy Scout name and your piano teacher will never claim you as a good student. Once you take a brand, make those that share your brand proud. There are few feelings that are as pleasing as working hard towards a goal with a group of people that you love and exceeding your goal. Competent coaches and teachers love to see their teams win and their students succeed.

I have no emotional attachment to what makes a person tick. I love Colorado. In a single drive to the grocery store it is not unusual for me to pass a couple hiking, a man on a motorcycle, passing a woman on a recumbent bike, who is pedaling while watching a hot air balloon over head and a big horned sheep on the roadside who is watching some kids climbing the side of a cliff. The interests are as diverse as our population is. It's all good! Everybody seems to wear a smile here. I just love watching Americans righteously enjoying America. The many things that we are passionate about never cease to amaze me. I love people who have passion for life, they pop. People with no passion tend to plop, like oatmeal spilling on the floor. We are all assigned something here on earth to learn and accomplish. We are each individually customized by God to do this. I think this is very important. The eye and the anus are each essential, but you can live without your eyes, so which body part is more important? At least throughout my career, I always justified being an ***hole with this statement. My friend says the body part she represents is a taste bud. Christ says we are all part of his body and important. Some parts are absolutely necessary, others could be sacrificed to keep the whole body alive, although the body won't be able to perform the way God designed it. We need to accept differences, respect the anus, the taste bud and the eye equally, and keep ourselves healthy so we can perform the work that we were put here to do. We need to eat, drink and be merry with the people that we love. Solomon says that this is our reward for all of the work we do under the sun. Everything else is vanity and chasing after wind he says.

Ride for your brands America, saddle up six days a week and give the seventh to God. That's another sin on the top-ten list that we have tended to ignore. The truth is that of the Ten Commandments, the rule that received the most verbiage was the sanctity of the Sabbath. If God changed His requirements for this one, I didn't get the Holy memo. Rest and honor God one day a week. This isn't a morbid day, this is a celebration. Make love, take a nap, take two, watch a football game, tell your children that you love them, go to Church, light a candle, climb a mountain, ski down it, then have a great meal. In everything you do acknowledge God and give Him thanks for your blessings and get ready to be at your work the next day as a happy steward of the gifts God has blessed you with. I didn't say be at your job, I said be at work. One feeds the other. Recreation or "re creating" is vital to keeping our Holy Spirit residing in a fleshly temple that isn't about to collapse around Him. To be a good person, one must first be a good animal. It is difficult to perform at ones best when one is injured, ill or in poor condition.

Fat is the result of one thing, consuming more than producing. It is the physical manifestation of taking more than your fair share and/or not giving up enough energy from the food you decide to consume. Collectively we are way too fat. Colorado is always the thinnest state in America, we stay fit. When I travel to Missouri and sit in a restaurant that has a smoking section and the average person is 40 pounds overweight, it is such a shocking contrast. We spend billions of dollars on weight loss products and programs. We are a nation in trouble when we need to spend extra billions to not eat and to get up and move! Do you realize how Bleeping crazy that has to sound to starving nations. We actually have television commercials that encourage children to go out and play an hour a day. I thought that is what we naturally did as kids. No wonder they hate us. If one has received unemployment benefits for over a year and they're still fat, one's benefits should be questioned.

The last brand is YOU! The way we became America was through a fighting spirit and collectively working to make individual dreams come true. We never became great by giving able bodied people handouts for long. We became great through living in accordance to God's will more often than not, and hard work. This is one nation under God and many of us believe in Him and behave accordingly. Unfortunately, this blessing is truly conditional and in jeopardy. We collectively create an aura that is either; neutral, positive or negative. Most of the world lives in poverty and squalor. Much of the world hates us! That is extremely negative energy aimed at you, me, our children, our parents, our neighbors, and friends. We need to respond with random acts of kindness, love, hope and charity. Remember, collective countenance rises with the elimination of each individual that has a low countenance, it's just simple math. But we need to turn this negative energy into positive energy or what is prophesied in the book of Revelations will come to pass. I once went to listen to the Dalai Lama speak in Denver in 1998. He responded to the question as to whether or not Armageddon was inevitable. He said that we were in control of this and that he didn't think it was necessary and that we were in the beginning of a spiritual revolution and that collectively we had the power to bring an awful existence into reality or to prevent it.

The Bible is clear; Christ will return and this will only happen after a horrible tribulation on earth. If the Dalai Lama is correct, we bring this on with our collective countenance, our collective energy and our collective level of love that flows through us each day versus the collective level of hatred. We need to be very careful of this INDIVIDUALLY! This means we need to follow God on our own, or pick the right people to follow and follow them. Create your own personal internal audience of great teachers. Add them to the family members and friends that fill out the existing internal audience that watches you perform your life each day. We all have an internal audience. When we get an A on an exam, our first thought is our parent's look of pride and sense of connection with the other students who took the class. These people give us feedback and inspiration internally in our positive mind chatter. These teachers get added to your internal audience with every class you attend, every book you read and every conversation that you participate in. We need to nurture what we love and learn to master our passions, control the passions that may hurt our souls and excel at the passions that express our souls. Excellence comes only through kung fu, time and energy, practice...hard work.

There is work America, if you want it. Hard work and a good countenance over time typically bring promotion. We need to look at how we define promotion. This should mean a change to experiencing greater joy at work. Not necessarily getting paid more and having more responsibility. It seems more in line with God's will to start at $7.50 an hour and work your way up, than to receive unemployment compensation while doing nothing but waiting for the "right job" to mysteriously appear.

There are days that we will work a 12 hour day at the ranch, during our busiest weekends of the summer these are challenging days. I drink 3 quarts of Gatorade on a typical work day and still lose an average of 6 pounds of sweat on that day. I make $7.50 an hour. I have no idea what each day will bring. I am thankful that in a few minutes I will transform from writer to cowboy. I earn more for being a cowboy than I earn from being a writer. Towards the end of my career, I regularly made over

$200,000 a year. I was happy then and I am happier now, but I hope that the tips are good today. We saddled over 50 horses on Saturday. I spent four and a half hours in the saddle and another four and a half hours leading a horse with a kid on it, at the picnics. I walked for four minutes, then took the child off the horse and put another on the horse and away we went. Between Saturday and Sunday I walked over six hours with one or two horses. I didn't waste a moment. This is where horse people are born! I spent six hours in the horse people delivery room as I was blessed to give many young children their first or second horseback ride in their lives.

My first delivery was actually to two adults, a married couple from Taiwan. They had never been on a horse until that day. They signed up for the trail ride offered as an activity at their company's picnic. I took them on the hour tour and as we began our decent down into the river bed I turned around and was kind of riding backwards as I guided them through the technical aspects of sitting in the saddle while going down or up steep grades. I saw an unusually horrified look on this lovely little woman from Taiwan and I turned around to see Mikey on the trail at the bottom. Mikey is an enormous Black Angus steer that would fit right in with the cast of characters that are ridden at the PBR. Fortunately, Mikey is as gentle as a dead pig, so I turned to the couple and said; "don't be afraid, he's a good guy". They looked at me as though I was crazy, they nodded and smiled. I lol'd as I thought to myself how insane that must sound, "Don't be afraid" while riding down a steep canyon for your first time on a horse heading straight into a 2,000 bull. But they did it! That was trust. I thanked God for the safe outcome, but I thanked Him more for giving me two human souls who put their lives in my hands and confronted a truly enormous challenge and succeeded. They were terrific followers, much more than I think we are asking for in our country from our workforce. That was truly blind followership. They were rightfully proud of themselves and their countenance soared. We came upon a rattlesnake sunning itself on this hot summer day, they got its picture. This was a perfect western experience and I was smiling for hours because of watching them be happy and grow. The remainder of the day was spent delivering young children into a horse life.

The look on a young child's face when they see the horse is the first indicator of whether or not this is a horse person. You cannot stop a horse person from being one and you cannot turn a non horse person into one. When I lift them up on the horse I can feel their fear and excitement. As we begin, I have to go through the parent taking picture thing, then we walk for three to five minutes and they study the experience, or talk, or just hold on for dear life and hope for a quick end to the ride. Then it sinks in. The natural horse person begs mom and dad for another ride and as you lift them onto the saddle, there is no fear, just joyful anticipation. This time the ride is lighter and typically, I'm asked if we can jog. I slowly jog and watch their eyes grow, as the speed increases and a horse person is delivered. I delivered a young girl from Pakistan, a young boy from Fort

Collins, a young girl from Loveland and many others, as their spirits connect with the spirit of the horse. This is worth every step I take and every kid I lift up on the saddle. The funny thing is that half of the children who became horse people that day began as the children who exhibited the most fear initially. The father of the girl from Pakistan forced her to get on the horse to experience it. She cried and was petrified. Most wimpy white parents would coddle their cowardly child and say, oh not today. And a coward is born. But this young girl came back for 5 more rides and trotted twice before the day was over. She felt great about herself, so did her father and so did I. To many children, this was just another summer picnic. To her, this was a life changing day. She became stronger. At the beginning, she was terrified, but she followed with faith because her father told her to do this, so it must be right, and I would protect her, so she must be safe, and she overcame her fear, and grew. When she's 36 years old in the workplace of America, I hope she follows with the same faith and trust. I pray that her whole life is abundantly filled with faith, trust and the love of her father. I know that she will always remember Saturday and I am thankful that I had a role. This is why I work. This is why my plants were the safest and most profitable of their type in the world. My job was to keep her safe; her job was to follow her father. That sums up this book's message about the job of the leader and the job of the follower. The leader also has to be able to motivate you to ride right into the bull, because of the promise of a good experience.

Most people are not horse people today. This is very sad. It has only been a century since the relationship of man and horse was typical and sacred. For most of history, man and horse are connected. Naturally designed to fit one another, man and horse forged history. There is no greater leader/follower relationship in life, than the relationship between man and horse. I love my two horses, Dixie and Liberty. We have great relationships. They are very different critters, but we work well as a team. They know that when it comes down to important stuff, I'm the boss. But we argue and challenge one another often. There is always a battle for the leadership role. Man's problem is that natural leaders are a breed that is extremely rare. More so than the number of horse people. But this battle for the leadership role continues even among people with no natural leadership qualities. I believe that the battle begins with the sin of coveting.

We love to talk about the Ten Commandments, but most of us don't know that there were two versions and most of us don't know that there were actually 613 commandments. Most of us don't know that the pomegranate is considered the Holy fruit because it has 613 seeds, find the Star of David on the fruit. Most of us don't honor the Sabbath, we don't consider coveting to be a no-no, yet both are on the same hit list as murder, adultery and theft. Most Christians that I meet, and know, don't really study the Old Testament. I think that Jesus made it clear during His ministry that the rules still apply. But these rules have to be applied as guided by the Holy Spirit that He indwelled in us through love and truth. There is a Jewish saying that Christians confess and Jews repent. This implies that Christian confession is hollow. I believe confession without repentance is nothing. Jesus said to His disciples after he had been crucified and raised, in Luke 24:47, "repentance for the forgiveness of sins should be proclaimed in His name." He didn't say that these 613 rules weren't sins anymore, nor did He say that forgiveness comes through confessions of sins. The Apostle Paul said that the wages of sin are death! Therefore we are in real trouble when we commit coveting or don't honor a Holy day each week. Not little trouble, big trouble. In fact if we love Jesus and believe His direction, we show this by following the rules. The two big rules on His hit list; love your Father with all of your heart and love your neighbor as you love yourself. His point was that if you follow those 2 rules you will adhere to most of the 613 rules. Jesus made some minor modifications. For example when stated that it isn't what we put into our mouth that causes us to sin, it is what comes out of our mouths that cause us to be counted as sinners. This is augmented by His direction to not eat things that causes your neighbor to sin or cause him to think that you sin. But go ahead, eat your lobster, have a ham sandwich, but make sure you give thanks to Jesus' Father. He always did.

Coveting is excessive mind chatter about wanting to have something that we don't have. There need not be an outward act or words spoken. As mentioned earlier, Joel Osteen says that we may not be able to control what is on each station on the channels of thought in our

163

minds, but we can control which station that we pay attention to. Watching internal channels depicting, images of something that we don't have, but want, is the sin of coveting. Physiologically this allows negative energy to flow through your body and brand your soul. Coveting always contributes to a degradation of countenance. Coveting can and does lead to other more obvious sins; adultery, theft, murder and blasphemy. Note that I said obvious sins, not serious sins. The sins on the top-ten list are weighted equally by God. The sin of coveting also affects one's ability to follow. Satan designed it this way to thwart our ability to work together and create happy lives. Coveting spurns jealousy and deceitfulness. Indeed, coveting is expressed through jealousy and deceitfulness. When this occurs with the relationship between you and your boss, or teacher, or coach, followership doesn't happen.

Creflo Dollar says that we need to change our mind-set. This is truly the only antidote for the sin of coveting. If we attack the acts and words of coveting, like we do adultery, our collective countenance will improve significantly without adding one material thing to our lives. We immediately become a little happier and haven't received anything. We have just let go of wanting. We won't struggle so much with following at work because we won't have our thoughts jaded with the jealousies we have towards those who, we perceive, have more power than we do. In fact having more power will lose its appeal and being the best we are supposed to be will become simpler. Wouldn't your life be different if you treated words from your children that express coveting, like you would treat racial slurs or cursing? Asking for that worthless new computer game would be the symptom, coveting would be the crime and punishment should follow. This isn't an American thought process, and because it isn't we have a society of those who unhappily want, instead of those who are happy with a truly abundant life.

As I walk through the streets of a typical town in Mexico and experience the sights and smells I get disgusted at how blind we are in this country, to how well we live. The people that we help at our ministry who don't have jobs live a life that is wonderful compared to their counterparts in small town Mexico, who work like dogs. We need to really understand the quality of life that the people have in the countries that we buy products from. We are enabling them to significantly improve their quality of life. But we don't pay them enough to live above poverty levels that we would consider tolerable here. We are not giving them anything, we require that they work extremely hard for the pennies an hour that we pay them. If they just move north, they can watch TV, and we'll feed them for free. Most Americans wouldn't even think of doing very hard physical labor, perfectly, for minimum wage. I earn minimum wage at the ranch and I hustle as do my co-workers, but I couldn't live the way I live on what I make as a wrangler. Nor could I do this kind of hard labor for 10-12 hours a day for many more years. This is another assignment from the Big Guy and a boyhood dream come true job. I love my life. It is about me, it is about you. It is that "one time in history" brand that says who

I am and what I contributed. Will my brand leave people with a smile or a frown, or worse, no reaction at all? What kind of reaction will your funeral bring to those in your life? This is more important than the size of your house, or the power of your job or the amount of your income. If you are going to covet, then covet great relationships that are full of fun and steeped in integrity and trust. Covet those who do God's work. Have self respect because you've earned it. Every precious day that we live, we should strive to make a difference in this world, or stay out of the way. We need to create a new balance in our great country. We are a people who over come, we will create a new world.

The concept of pride can be difficult to grasp, like the concept of coveting or ego. We are proud to be Americans, we want to take pride in our work and be proud of our children. We need to be competent, but we must keep our ego in check. We want a better life for our children, but coveting is a sin. We want to have pride in our work, yet we need to give the credit and glory to God. The Yin Yang symbol is alive and well. Balance is required to please God and maintain a healthy countenance. The difference between good pride and being prideful is typically obvious. Wanting to be competent is a good thing, being egotistical is usually considered a bad thing. The yin yang symbol represents a balance of opposites, so we need to maintain a happy balance of being proud versus being prideful. We want a good life and abundance for our children, but excessive wanting is a major sin.

Imagine if the media exposed a politician for being caught in the act of coveting as opposed to the act of adultery. Don't laugh! This may be in your future. Our new Chinese politicians have been schooled in keeping their comrades living without, as equals. Not wanting is essential for living with next to nothing if you want to live happily. They don't look at it as coveting control, but it kind of is. We'll need to start to condition us minions with television, You Tube etc. There will be a new show on television depicting the special Covet Squad in the NYPD, or the sequel, The Poor Countenance Unit. The truth is the opposite of want, is fulfillment. The opposite of lack, is full. If we stop coveting, the opposite is being thankful. Thankful people have positive countenances. Positive people produce good works. Positive energy heals; relationships, physical ailments, natural weather patterns and the earth's propensity to quake or erupt. Positive people create, negative people destroy, those who live in the middle, experience mediocrity; cold oatmeal dropping on the floor, plop! For most of us that is sufficient and good. Most of us are not stars. We don't create great things or break world records. Instead we work hard and try to be good to the people in our lives. We all experience similar life dramas and dysfunctional family life scenarios.

The vast majority of us do not consider the act of coveting as serious as the acts of adultery, killing or theft. In truth, we don't even give it the value of misdemeanor. I truly don't know anyone who considers not honoring the Sabbath to be significant. We have the notion that going to church covers the Sabbath thing. Going to church is not anything like a day of complete rest. The statements in the Bible about the Sabbath don't even mention any required worship. The denominational church systems that man has created have changed the rules. I'm not a fan of our modern day scribes, Pharisees and Sadducees. I love several of our best television ministers; Joyce Meyer, Joel Osteen, John Hagee, Joseph Prince and I watch historical shows regularly. Why wait until Sunday. Instead of another re-run of Seinfeld, turn on a 30 minute sermon just one day a week, give it a try. One of my favorite songs is Wind Up by Jethro Tull. He's not the kind you have to wind up on Sunday. Worship is different than learning through a sermon, but it is required. Worship has to include sacrifice. We've stopped killing animals on the altar but we are supposed to tithe. Most of us would prefer to write a check than kill a ram. But one or the other has to happen to complete the works that God has assigned to all of us. Show me in the Bible where we were supposed to stop sacrifice. I volunteered for 5 hours at the food bank this morning. I consider that my active prayer and physical tithe. Worship however best fits your spiritual needs and beliefs, but worship. I hate to sit in church and listen to a bore, although I occasionally like the rituals of several denominations. My favorite pew is on the back of a horse or on the chairlift. But worship is not rest either. Pray, sing, shout, give praise and glory to God every day. Tell Satan to go *Bleep* himself, yell at him, curse him, don't listen to him, this is also worship.

One may argue that becoming a Christian means that we are free from the law. We are supposed to add the element of, letting the law be our goal, our conscience is our guide and common sense should be applied to prove that we are followers of Christ by being fair and forgiving. We shouldn't be stoning people for acts of adultery, but I would rather be stoned than endure what Tiger Woods had to everyday. We are supposed to forgive 7 X 70 times. We are supposed to throw the stone only if we have no sin. We are supposed to keep the logs out of our own eye and let our neighbor worry about the spec in his eye. These are words that Jesus spoke. He talked about a difference in how to treat the law, but he followed the law perfectly until he healed a crippled man on a Sabbath. In John 5, he really throws down the gauntlet when he proclaims that he is the Son of God and that judgment has been given to Him. He makes it clear that He is the Judge and Moses is the prosecuting attorney. He says in verses 45 & 46; "Do not think that I will accuse you before the Father; the one who accuses you is Moses, in whom you have set your hope."

"For if you believed Moses, you would believe Me; for he wrote of Me". Jesus was born in fulfillment of Moses' words. Jesus lived as a perfect Jew. If we plan to imitate Him, we are essentially striving to live according to Jewish law, as He did day after day. The real difference between the thought process of a pre Christian Jew and a Christian is the element that Christ taught us about the Holy Spirit living in each of us. He told us God's voice can be heard by each of us if we listen. We are forgiven if we repent. We repent to show that we are sorry for our sinning and we won't do it again. Finally we are supposed to forgive and let vengeance be His. These are huge differences and this makes one a Christian, when one believes this is truly the truth. Jesus is the son of Mary and God and His words express what God wants us to know and follow. But we are still human animals and we will still trespass, hopefully less and less as one matures and one's relationship to God deepens. Meanwhile we have to endure one another's life learning curves as we try to work together. Remember the yin yang symbol, we cannot escape the fact we are half good and half evil. Simply stay on the path daily and your future will be secure even though your present may suck. But go to work every day.

There is a difference between being a good worker and being a good employee. A good worker does his tasks efficiently, safely, with integrity. The first thing about being both a good worker and a good employee is attendance. This is a huge issue with every start to every business day. Who didn't show up? A good worker and good employee are always there. A good worker does more than standard all of the time at every task he undertakes. A good worker can be a real pain in the butt on some very serious levels and still be a productive asset. A good employee supports company policy and practices. A good employee always follows the rules, doesn't argue with peers or superiors, doesn't gossip, tells the truth and goes the extra mile for everybody. A good employee may be slow at tasks or unable to understand as readily as others or may not be able to produce as much as some great workers but they produce enough to stay employed. But a good employee is a joy to have on the team, even if they may require closer supervision. Over time, a team of great workers but bad employees will lose to a team of mediocre workers who are great employees. But we should all strive to be both if we want to be a good follower.

Be a believing follower. Believe in your God, believe in your family, believe in your company, believe in your teachers and most importantly believe in yourself! You are Holy, you are anointed and your work is important, as is your purpose here. Ride for your brands. Have fun and live abundantly.

Chapter 6

To Leaders:

Don't Shtoink the Help

"Potent leadership is a matter of being aware of what is happening in the group and acting accordingly. Specific actions are less important than the leader's clarity or consciousness. That is why there are no exercises or formulas to ensure successful leadership.

Potency cannot be calculated or manipulated, nor is it a matter of trying to look good."

John Heider

The above quote from John Heider's, "The Tao of Leadership" sums up why I am not in favor of sending people to leadership classes who have no natural leadership talent. There are no rules that will ensure success as a leader. There are some rules that if you break I can guarantee you that your potency will be reduced or worse. My father Herb gave me two rules about relating to my fellow man. He said never mess with a man's woman or his pay. There is one significant do; "do unto others as you would have them do unto you", love your people! The remaining leadership rules are don'ts. Most of us will break some of these rules from time to time, many will probably not agree with some, but in my experience if you avoid the things I'm warning you about, your relationships will be more productive.

When it comes to the workplace I will tell you that nothing impacts a person's potency at work more than becoming romantically involved with somebody at work. Even when the relationship is honorable, you will both sacrifice potency and respect. I did a study back in the 80's about people who had relationships at work to determine the average amount of time that was devoted to attending to the relationship while on the job. There were no emails or cell phones in those days. These were not illicit affairs. These were honorable dating or marriage. The study included 100 people who became involved at work. The average time reported was just a little under two hours when the relationship began, down to less than ½ an hour to those who were married. I'm sure that there have been studies since the advent of texting and emails, but the truth is that an inordinate amount of time gets devoted to relationship building when people date at work. This time stolen from your company to "git some" never goes on without the rumor mill getting cranked up and people watching as your relationship grows. This becomes how you are identified by most of your coworkers, not what kind of worker or employee you are, but you're shtoinking so and so. Never get angry at the well nourished rumor mill when it is you who are feeding it. Don't blame people for invading your personal life, when you open it up to them in the first place.

The situation worsens if the relationship involves a boss and a subordinate. The truth is most leaders have charisma, and power can be an aphrodisiac, because of this, leaders often have opportunity for romance that non leaders don't. Be very aware of this and calculate the consequences before you let loose with that first flirtatious compliment. The situation gets very unpredictable and fragile when the relationship is illicit. There are some happy endings to love stories at work. In my 18 years in senior management, I've seen very few happy endings compared to unhappy endings. From the point of view of the head guy at a business, office romance is always a pain in the ass. Accusations of favoritism, discrimination and harassment often ensue. When one person has a problem or goes on vacation, then typically two people have a problem or are gone. If the budding romance involves a boss and subordinate then it usually becomes necessary to try to accommodate the couple by reassigning one of them. This always causes problems in these departments. Who ends up repaying the company when two people spend two hours of company time each day to invest their time in one another? Most of your co-workers resent this and your potency is always affected. When a marriage fails between two co-workers, it is always a disaster. This happens to over 50% of the marriages.

If the relationship is illicit, it rarely stays truly a secret for long, nobody can predict the outcome. If Murphy's Law holds true, the explosion of discovery will always come at the worse time. If people at work know that you're dipping your pen in the company ink well, your potency gets totally destroyed and if you are a boss you may get fired. Not necessarily if you're the President of the United States, but under most circumstances you could be fired. This doesn't say anything about how much mind chatter is now devoted to your affair, versus to your business affairs. When you are in an illicit affair your whole life goes out of balance, whether or not it ever gets discovered. I know from my own experience and from having responsibility for Human Resources departments for two decades that people in affairs always develop problems at work and home. Their reputation always suffers, others always suspect. True love shows, so does true guilt. When you look for romance at work the only thing you end up courting is disaster. DON'T DO IT!

The next great killer of potency is talking negatively about anybody at anytime, unless it includes the individual in question with the appropriate Human Resource support in a professional setting. We expect confidentiality when we visit our doctor or lawyer. This same level of privacy and professionalism should be expected when one becomes a supervisor of others. This is very difficult to control over time, but the consequences of bad mouthing any subordinate to another person is a monster trust buster. If you talk about one person, then everybody will rightfully assume that when it is to your advantage, you will talk about them too. Negative talk breeds negative countenance. As a leader your job is countenance control. You sabotage your own potency when you can't keep yourself from gossiping. I had a rule that if one employee wanted to talk negatively about a coworker, unless there were harassment issues or other confidentiality concerns, I insisted that we include the complained about employee in the conversation. If you want to say something bad about somebody, say it in front of them.

Imbibing with subordinates is also a real killer of leadership potency. As an iron pourer back in the 70's, we all drank and got high after work together. In those days management provided a trash can full of ice and beer below the time clock at the foundry I worked at in Guilford, Connecticut. We all drank a quart of beer and fired up a doobie at lunch each day under the bridge by the plant in Hopedale, Massachusetts, then we returned to work pouring 2,800 degree iron. When I was interviewed for my first corporate job after I graduated in 1977, the Corporate Recruiter took me out for a Milwaukee German dinner and drinking was part of the test. The day after, the V. P. of Personnel asked how much I could drink. I drank a lot, I got the job. In the 80's, stopping with the team after work at the local watering hole was a regular occurrence. Colorado was quite the party state back in the 70's 80's and 90's. I had a great time and I enjoyed the camaraderie. I did millions of dollars worth of business entertaining back then.

I quit drinking in 1995. I have never looked back. My quality of life has just continued to improve. Even open heart surgery and a total of 8 operations on my knees, shoulder and neck, through my athletic injuries, haven't tempted me to return to drinking. If I'm told I will have to have another open heart operation however, I will book a flight and call a dozen buddies and drink a few beers. But until then I don't plan to drink again. I don't enjoy drinking situations, so entertaining isn't my thing anymore. I really see the impact that drinking has on people. I can tell if somebody is hung over, or needing a drink at 4:30. I can smell alcohol on somebody's breath if they had a drink within the last 24 hours. Because I'm a dud, most of my coworkers stopped inviting me to stop after work or to weekend parties and my potency at work soared. After the death of a friend in 1997, I made it a personal policy to not socialize with coworkers unless it was work or sales related. I stuck to that policy until I retired in 2008. I can say that this made my life so much simpler at work. I can also say that when an employee has a drinking problem it always affects his or her work. If you are the boss and have a drinking problem, you won't be the boss very long if you don't get help and quit. Once you quit, your performance will skyrocket, your life will get better. There is nothing greater that you could do for your company, your family and yourself than to solve a drinking problem. If you don't have a problem with drinking, you are much better off to NEVER drink with your subordinates anyway.

Those subordinates and coworkers that are not included in the partying, often feel excluded from the team. In some instances coworkers are, rightfully angered over having to work with hung over people who are the boss's buddies. This is a real problem in dangerous industrial settings. How do you think it will feel to have to send a subordinate out to take a drug and alcohol test after an industrial accident, when you bought the booze the previous night? Good bye career. I just heard another CNN study that recommended that you need to party with your subordinates to build relationships. This doesn't surprise me in light of the way that the pendulum swings in life. But I still say it is safer to separate business and pleasure.

Don't play "good guy-bad guy", to your subordinates about your boss. This is common and causes a significant loss in potency. If you want your people to follow you, then don't blame your boss for the unpleasing rules, schedules, assignments and decisions that have to be made. You wanted to be the leader, then don't hand off the hard stuff. Sometimes we can have a horrible boss who really makes bad decisions, never the less, wasting too much talk and mind chatter about the bad stuff will only negatively impact collective countenance. Your people will see who the culprit is when things go wrong, you don't have to point the finger upward. You only risk getting it chopped off. You'll make mistakes too. A leader should avoid creating a division between his boss and his subordinates. It may be very difficult to effectively maneuver at times, but understand that there will be consequences from both your boss and your subordinates if you play games.

The chain of command is a great concept, but I haven't seen this in action in corporate America in decades. Today it is kind of a "rope of command". Intertwined closely are the various interest representatives to guide the business and direct activities. You may be a plant manager, but first you answer to your customers, then your corporate boss, and his boss's boss. Of course there is corporate human resources, corporate accounting, corporate safety, corporate engineering all woven into a rope of gray. Black and white leaders will not survive. In today's business environment you need to be a strong strand in that rope and not let the violations of people directing your people upset your countenance. Change the thought channel and cooperate.

There were very few actions that enraged me more than when my boss placed people in my organization. The second action that chapped my butt was when a superior went around me to a subordinate. This happens all of the time, everywhere. This sets the manager up for failure if it gets out of control. I had a work habit of trying to say hello to everybody each day. When this included three shifts of over 300 people, one has to move quickly and set a pattern. I've had co-workers tell me that they could set their watch by when I passed by such and such, machine each day. This opens the door to conversations with everybody. Therefore, I stepped around several layers of management at times. I was always very aware of what we were talking about, I wanted there to be an open door, but I NEVER gave direction to or permission to, some other manager's subordinate, while on my rounds. If there were issues to be discussed, then I would get their supervisor and/or a representative from H.R. After a while everybody felt more at ease with my presence. Supervisors, managers and operators learned my rules, therefore, people knew that I respected the chain of command and they didn't "go around" their boss to me, and I didn't do it either. Once the head guy respects the chain of command and makes this a common practice, every leader's potency improves. Just because your superiors will violate this, as will the non-rock moving corporate people who are there to help, that doesn't mean you shouldn't insist on the chain of command working below you. Breaking the chain of command always becomes a problem if it becomes a habit. Your boss will do this to you, it will cause pain, so don't let the mind chatter get out of control and remember this when it is your turn to supervise supervisors. When you, as a manager, "go around" a subordinate supervisor, you decrease their leadership potency. Remember that your potency increases as your subordinate's potency increases, and the reverse is true as well.

Don't SHTOINK with a man's pay! This is an area where most make mistakes, and these mistakes are very rarely forgiven. NEVER PROMISE A RAISE. Never tell a subordinate that you are going to try to get them a raise. Never tell them that your boss has turned it down or corporate turned it down. When you blame some other entity for a man's pay level, then you must give that entity the credit when raises are awarded. You, as a leader, become a paper tiger, worthless to your people. The vast majority of companies have very clear policies and practices regarding pay and raises. If you have people whose pay you control, know the policies and practices inside out. Use them to motivate your people the best you can, with what you have. No policy or practice is perfect, but most are very workable. All policies will hurt you if you make a mistake or communicate incorrectly. Your relationship with your subordinate will forever be tarnished if you promise a raise that you don't deliver on. NEVER tell a person about a raise until you personally look into their pay envelope and calculate that the raise you submitted was the raise that actually came through on the check. When you hand that person their check, explain exactly why YOU decided that the level of raise was commensurate with their performance. The raise, the evaluation, the check should be as close to the same moment as possible.

When you become a new boss, whether promoted into the job or hired in as a boss, there will be about 30% of your workforce that will want to talk to you about a raise. Just be an anus to them all, fairly and courteously. Even your best friend will ask you for a raise as soon as you get promoted over him or her. Friendships change when the relationship changes at work. This is one of those hard lessons that we learn as we climb the ladder, this is what my grandfather was talking about. Understand that as you grow as a leader, these relationships have to change. They have to mature. Your role as a leader is to point the way to improved performance and countenance for everybody in your charge, and motivate them to grow as adults. When you are promoted, this can be difficult to successfully change these relationships into a boss/subordinate dynamic, from equal and friends (or maybe enemies). But since you are now the boss, it is your job to facilitate this. As a follower, it is your job to accommodate this. Do not avoid rebuilding all of these relationships, one transaction at a time. One Emotional Bank Account Deposit at a time.

Don't ever talk about your pay or your bonus in front of anyone but your boss. We are a jealous creature and all subordinates feel that their boss gets more than they do. Don't rub it in, don't look for sympathy, don't complain, don't brag, never discuss your pay. Nothing you say about your own pay can help your leadership potency.

Leaders should care for their people above everything else. There is a Proverb that I have used throughout my career. In fact, my retirement watch was inscribed with Proverb 27:23 & 24. "Be sure you know the condition of your flocks, give careful attention to your herds; for riches do not endure forever; and a crown is not secure for all generations." This is your #1 job as a leader. Everything else comes after you know the flock is safe and secure. Jesus said in Mathew 20: 26-28. "Whoever wishes to be great among you shall be your servant, and whoever wishes to be first among you shall be your slave." The greatest leader will be the greatest server. You should look at your job as being each subordinate's personal coach. When you approach your work this way, making sure to always talk about their daily score, your people will follow you. Be firm, fair and consistent. Before the sun goes down each day, make sure your emotional bank account balances are in order with each of your subordinates. If you have a debit balance, make sure you rebuild this account as soon as you can, before the days first break. Don't let your people go to a break with resentment on their mind, when you caused it! Timing is always an important variable to consider. A leader should love his/her people, direct their activities and respect them like one respects one's mother. A leader gives regular, thoughtful feedback. The leader administers praise or punishment as performance and behavior warrant.

Work to make sure that your people get the biggest piece of the pie that is fair to the team, fair to the company and fair to the individual. We are always in business to make a profit. This is our first priority and how profit is managed should be shared with all team members. Business protocol very likely may prohibit you from sharing financial results, you may not know yourself. There is only one reason for this kind of behavior. The people at the top make too much and they take it from the hardest working people at the bottom or from their suppliers.

If a company cannot honestly share what their profit numbers are, something is wrong. Honesty is one of those principles that are timeless. If the company cannot live by that principle, they cannot be trusted as a supplier, an employer or community member. British Petroleum lied to everyone about the amount of oil that was spewing into the gulf. When most scandals break, it is the act of "cover up" which usually gets people in the most trouble. This is honesty in action or not. As a leader, you want to be constant and consistent about getting your people what is fair. When you live this way, your people will see this and your potency will soar. Their loyalty will be your greatest asset as a leader. If you can make work fun, your teams will win. Your job is to bring honor to your people's work. You shine the light of praise on your team, or they will live in the dark. You can make flipping that burger fun and honorable. Or you can make it a living hell for the burger flipper if you are a poor boss. Never tell your subordinate that you are "working on their raise". Work on it if they deserve it, but do it behind the scenes. You create a huge amount of mind chatter for an employee who is left hanging while waiting for you to make something happen. I have actually paid subordinates out of my pocket when my boss reversed or procrastinated on a raise decision. My word was more important to me than my money. This always turned out to be money well invested.

There is nothing that most leaders can do today that can significantly impact pay practices. If you own your business, this is something to think about. A person cannot live on minimum wage. Minimum wage is typically paid to the lowest skilled people for doing the hardest jobs. Minimum wage is also reserved for service jobs like flipping burgers, waiting on tables, simple assembly and redundant busy work. There is a place for a minimum wage, but we are competing in a global market where the average hourly labor rate is significantly below our minimum wage. The global workforce does not have the working conditions that we enjoy, or the cafeteria plans of benefits to augment their pay that ObamaCare requires and Americans have come to expect. This cost advantage enables the Chinese manufacturers to produce a product that cost less than its American counterpart even when the cost of freight from China is factored in. These factories in China don't have the pollution controls or product safety levels that we expect in the products that we buy. As Americans we need to understand that our purchases are really votes. They reveal what your beliefs are. I hate to sound old fashioned, but; "Buy American"! When you buy American, you say that you believe that a fair days pay should get you a fair quality of life. Your American choice says that you believe that pollution controls and our environment are important; you say the same thing about safe working conditions and employment laws that protect our people. Most importantly you say that you want your American money to go to Americans. Be a living example.

Don't lie! This sounds childish to address, but dishonesty is a real potency killer. There are times that truth cannot be shared; when you're going through an acquisition, re-organization, new product creation, but usually truth should always be the order of the day. Your job as a leader is to enlighten, to facilitate and direct your group's activities towards success. Be as honest as is politically correct. Seriously question working for a liar or somebody who asks you to lie. Don't make stuff up and don't omit important details. The only power we have is in our words, God makes them magical when you spice your words with truth and kindness. Don't share confidential information with anyone. Never talk to anyone about any personnel or disciplinary actions that you take with your subordinates, don't lie about it; just don't share it.

Don't hand off training your subordinates, to another subordinate. This is common for supervisors to give the job of training new people to lead people or other operators. Obviously, these people need to assist in the learning process, but the initial instruction about tasks and instruction about company rules and policies should be yours. There is an old martial arts saying; "He who teaches, learns twice." This is very true. As the day gets busy, it is easy to leave the training to a trusted subordinate. When you do that, who do you think the new person looks to for leadership? People imprint too.

My last leadership rule is; try to catch people doing the right thing and make an issue about it. Many bosses try to catch people doing the wrong things and then they address the wrong action. Try focusing on catching people doing excellent things and address that. You will be amazed at how many great things you "catch". You will also find that the more you comment about right things, the fewer wrong things will be done.

These are the big basics. I can also say with certainty that I have learned all of these rules the hard way, some of them I've learned the hard way more than once. I have also corrected these mistakes throughout my career and I can say that living in accordance to these rules yields positive results. I worked for a company and we had a senior vice president who had rules for everything pertaining to running a manufacturing business in our industry, the vast majority of his rules were great. I learned a lot about the tasks required to be a successful General Manager through memorizing these rules. But this is a book about followership, not general managership.

The Universe grows us humans like a terrarium provides an environment suitable for growing vegetation.

Solomon says, in Ecclesiastes, that there is an appointed time for everything. In chapter three verses nine through thirteen, Solomon says that God has made everything appropriate in its time. There is nothing better for us than to rejoice, do good and enjoy the good in our labor. When you become a leader, God is blessing you with souls to lead to help them grow and rejoice, this will give you joy in your work. This is not insignificant to God. The job of being a leader is huge. When this happens, it is your time to lead. I heard of a study once in the 70's that said that a person devotes about 10% of his or her mind chatter to his or her boss. The better the boss, the less mind chatter, the worse the relationship with one's boss, the higher the percentage of time was devoted to mind chatter. Be a good boss. Make sure that 10% is positive. Collective countenance can only improve when mind chatter is positive more than negative. When you become a boss, you are then judged as a boss. You're held to a higher standard. When you are a good follower, you hold yourself to the highest possible standard, God's. All bosses have to be followers as well. Be a good example to your people. Be the subordinate that you want to have. Behave according to your own expectations for being a good worker and employee.

YOUR job is to step on slugs, and reward the ants and locust. My friend who told me that the people who need this book most, don't buy this kind of book, is right. Therefore this is really a book to you, the leader, in a backdoor kind of way. We need to really examine our pay practices, our hiring practices and our firing practices. Leaders need to focus on making sure we are all efficiently doing value added work. Those that don't contribute enough to justify their pay should face correction, either loss of job or lower pay. Middle managers, engineers and sales people need to truly study their own work. For those who don't, your bosses should. But you leaders must lead. The most important job that you have is moving your people to the Promised Land. Nobody ever got to the Promised Land riding on the backs of slugs. Everybody in America has taken steps to control costs during these last few years. All organizations have been examined for saving opportunities. Times are tough, our competition is tougher.

Leaders lose their jobs too. This is especially important for you to grow during this time off. Don't take leadership skills development lightly. These skills always need to be worked on. Get involved and work on these skills. Take classes, use the internet, lead a church project or become a scout master, coach a soccer team. Your spiritual job is to help others grow, water them, shed light on what's happening, reward them for doing well, punish them for not living up to their potential or for laziness, stupidity, disrespectful, dishonest or irresponsible behavior or actions. Love them all and stay detached. Bit by bit, opportunity for leadership will find you. God uses leaders for His purpose. Stay close to Him and you'll have a job soon. Everything in life is this way. If you stop working on your marriage, or your profession, or your physical fitness, or your spiritual fitness, you'll lose your edge. You'll miss the opportunity God has coming your way if you're taking a nap or watching television. That opportunity goes by and is taken by somebody who is preparing for it.

Chapter 7

To managers

"Management is a bottom line focus: How can I best accomplish certain things? Leadership deals with the top line: What are the things that I want to accomplish? In the words of both Peter Drucker and Warren Bennis, "Management is doing things right; leadership is doing right things." Management is efficiency in climbing the ladder of success; leadership determines whether the ladder is leaning against the right wall."

"You can quickly grasp the important difference between the two if you envision a group of producers cutting their way through a jungle with machetes. They're the producers, the problem solvers. They're cutting down the underbrush, clearing it out."

"The managers are behind them, sharpening their machetes, writing policy and procedure manuals, holding muscle development programs, bringing in improved technologies and setting up working schedules and compensation programs for machete wielders."
(Stephen Covey101)

The word "manage" come from the Italian word maneggiare, which means to handle. My definition for manage is to ensure right action is taken at the appropriate time, to meet entity needs. According to Peter Drucker (1909-2005), the basic tasks of management are innovation and marketing. According to Wikipedia, the definition of manage is; "the organization and coordination of the activities of an enterprise in accordance with certain policies and in achievement of clearly defined objectives." However, we all know that one can "manage on one's own", so it need not be an organization that is organized or coordinated. It may simply be the many activities that an individual has to undertake to maintain a healthy balance in life. The task of managing is to organize, coordinate and act. It usually helps to have reminders, prompts and boundaries with which to help us decide how and when to act. These prompts and reminders usually come in the form of a system that helps guide these action decisions. If one manages a system that provides timely truth, one can lead people to undertake tasks to meet the organizations needs, to fulfill the organizations goals. Timely truth is critical to making all decisions.

The concept of "multi-tasking" is far from new. Although the phrase may be somewhat recent, man has been multi-tasking forever. People can be extremely busy doing tasks all day, every day, yet get nothing of value accomplished because they don't do the things that move the rock. People in organizations can easily become slaves to systems instead of followers of principals and generators of profit. In fact, we take pleasure in knowing our jobs and doing them well. This repeated activity process builds us a comfort zone in our daily habits that eventually can become a zone we defend and protect. We like doing this task and don't like doing that one. We hold tightly to the tasks we like, we avoid tasks that we don't like and we covet tasks that we don't get an opportunity to do. Almost everybody covets power to some degree. This simple scenario represents a typical person in an organization. We need to understand why tasks aren't "liked".

Task satisfaction, like most things falls into a bell curve. There are tasks that are great to do, there are tasks that are hard, uncomfortable and filthy to do, and there are a whole bunch of tasks in the middle. There are tasks that require a great deal of skill or education or both. There are tasks that a monkey could do. There are tasks that a "little ole lady" could do and others that would exhaust an ox. The distribution of work requires the separation of tasks.

Division of labor was the key difference in Henry Ford's assembly lines, from the previous methods employed to manufacture stuff. He separated the manual tasks and divided them by a number of people that would enable each person to do a relatively equal and small amount of work. If the longest task took three minutes then the assembly line could produce one car every three minutes or 20 cars an hour. If you wanted more cars you could do one of two things or both. You could re-divide the labor and add enough people to drive the longest task time down. If you add four people, the longest task may now be two minutes or 30 cars an hour. Or you could use the same number of people and work more hours (overtime), or you could do variations of both. A manager decides mathematically how to divide the labor and the hours to minimize the overall labor costs while maximizing the daily production.

As an industrial/methods engineer in the 70's, I worked briefly in the tail light assembly department for Buick, in Flint, Michigan while attending GMI. Our job was setting work standards, after we established work methods. Then we balanced the assembly line to meet the needs of sales. The department superintendant was constantly demanding that we streamline the tasks each time we re-balanced the line. The Union was constantly scrutinizing the standards and fighting for more time. The Union wanted the tasks to take the longest time possible so the company could hire more people which would provide more union dues. This was counter to any company's goal of profitability. When activities go against the generation of profit, these actions put the business at risk. The market always sets the price. It is the manager's job to make sure that the costs to manufacture and sell are less than the price that the market dictates. Labor costs are a function of total number of employees and the amount each one gets paid. It is always in everybody's interest to have the fewest number of people doing the greatest number of the correct tasks using the most efficient methods.

Each time we make a hiring decision, we are making a million dollar decision. We will pay a person well over a million dollars if they work for a lifetime and if things don't work out, then a company can spend well over a million dollars in legal costs and punitive damages if there is a law suit. However most managers simply hire people to address problems or increase production and they don't undertake sufficient due diligence in selecting the best fit. The lower the person gets paid, the quicker the hiring process. But we really shortchange ourselves by under paying our people. I'm not saying to not negotiate the best value, but to set the relationship up with an imbalance will only be a de-motivator. We need our followers to believe. We want them to follow out of love and trust. Nobody trusts anyone who cheats us. There are methods that can simply and effectively ensure that the job role is paid a fair market price for the skill and difficulty of the position. There are countless ways to implement an incentive system that rewards behaviors and performance that contribute to profit. If you want full time dedicated people who follow enthusiastically, then you need to pay a fair price for skills and effectiveness. Share profits commensurate with level of risk. And pay for performance through an incentive system that enables people to be rewarded for success and above average contribution.

The market sets the price for wages and salaries. If we are insisting on competing in a global economy then we have to really understand that our skills are worth significantly less in third world countries than we get paid for here. This isn't a cost of living adjustment, like if you move from New York City to Hutchinson, Kansas. This is an enormous standard of living adjustment. There is no doubt in my mind that this recession is worse than a depression. It is actually an equalization that we are experiencing. This is the "Great Global Equalization". The overall standard of living on earth is probably on the rise. We Americans need to re-create our systems of paying all of us. And we need to manage our systems, not be slaves to our systems.

We need to seriously look at the productivity impact that unions have on our country. We have more than enough environmental, employment, safety and ethical laws in place to protect our working people. We don't need contra-organizations sabotaging us while they steal money directly out of the pockets of its members and out of the pockets of the American people who have to pay inflated prices for our products. Not to mention the fact that American companies shut down American operations, and move overseas to avoid dealing with Unions. We need to stop negotiating for pay rates and make sure that pay is skill and impact based.

When we have designed incentive systems in my past, we have found that skill based pay combined with gain sharing, create a work force attitude that is enthusiastically charged to perform. There are many things to be considered after the entity has become comfortably profitable. The first thing to consider is how much profit is smart to distribute to the team who earned it. One must consider the pay that a wage unit is worth, the base pay for the market price of the entry level skill value. On our ranch, the lowest, easiest job to learn is cleaning up manure, but we don't have a person who just does that. It is part of my job, the Wrangler. We shovel poop, and transport the manure to a designated area driving a tractor. We need to know first aid & CPR, we need to be able to handle, train and control most horses. We need to understand how a multitude of tack combinations work, bits, halters, bridals, saddles and more. We are the people who tack up the horses, groom them and feed them. We need to understand topography and orientation methodologies. We take up to 10 horses and riders per wrangler onto mountain trails. This requires that we can communicate well with a variety of people from all over the world. We must be able to ride well and having had some roping experience and basic shoe repair skills are a plus. We work 12 hours shifts in the 90+ degree heat and in the Colorado cold. This position pays $7.50 an hour. Compare that to making $15 an hour for loading flat sheets of corrugated cardboard into machines at a specific rate per hour and quality level. The work is equally hard, yet the variety of skills and athleticism needed to be a successful wrangler far exceed that of a die-cutter operator. Unless the operator also understands and can perform quality tasks, scheduling tasks, labor reporting tasks, training tasks and die design concepts. I know that it is easier to teach scheduling to people who understand English. It is easier to teach statistical process control techniques to a person with math skills and it is easier to manage your plant with people who have a real understanding of business and accounting, which is also easier to teach to people with math and English skills. But we hire people fresh off the boat and turn them loose to load machines while others attend to the statistical reporting, accounting, scheduling and design needs.

President Obama gave a report to the nation and tried to address the disappearance of the middle class and the nightmare that the American dream has become. He tried to maximize the great job that he's done bringing our troops home and touched on the problems of our economy. He still had an election to win at the time so he certainly didn't want to tell us the truth about the actual fate that we have waiting for us if the current trends don't reverse themselves. But the current trends will not change unless we reverse the job loss to third world countries and the erosion of our manufacturing base. This won't change.

Therefore, we need to change our mind-sets about what that American dream is. There has to be a true paradigm change in our values. This is an individual choice and responsibility. Our America will still be "America the Beautiful", it will hopefully be the land of green products and processes and the home of brave happy productive people who fulfill their destinies. That may not include a home with a mortgage and four bedrooms, three baths with a two car garage.

We spend so much money on physical fitness in this country. Most of the regulars at these gyms could get a comparable workout with manual labor. Winston Churchill built walls with bricks. True, he drank like a fish and smoked like a chimney, but he was a great diplomatic leader. He worked on strengthening by doing skilled work, instead of spinning. Maybe!

It is very important for us to honor all honest, quality labor. This requires a pay level that enables a responsible American a safe, secure quality of life. I'm not saying give money away. I am saying teach people to have a value that is commensurate with their pay. Have significantly fewer overpaid people and have responsible total employees. The team would be made up of people who can really "multi-task" proudly because they are trained to do many jobs. Take the money we spend on these managers and divide it among the "Total Employees".

We need to be sincere about the elimination of slavery on this planet. Not just pay it lip service in your church and school. We have taken a stand against blood diamonds. Shouldn't we take a stand against masked slavery? Slavery can also be a mind-set. People who feel that they are exploited and abused live in an attitude of slavery. When an honest hard working American has to work two menial jobs to make ends meet, there is very little freedom left in the day. Personally I'd rather pick cotton, live in a shack on a ranch with decent food and a kind master, than work two jobs and never have anything but bills to pay and fear of losing one of the jobs. There is nothing written in any holy book that I've read that says slavery is wrong. Treatment of slaves is addressed, but whether or not there should be slaves is never addressed. In fact it is clear that Jesus accepted slavery and we do today, only it isn't politically correct to suggest that. We simply don't have to watch the people put your track shoes together, in 100 degree heat for dollars a day. These shoes sell for more than these people earn a month working 180 hours. New Balance still makes shoes in America, hooray for them! It can be done. I've been through their plants in Maine, they are clean productive plants with home grown Americans working there and making a living.

I haven't invented anything, but I have taken other people's ideas and had tremendous success with them. My first crusade in my career was skill-based pay. In America one can easily find the market values for any skill set and experience level. In Denver, we have an organization called the Mountain States Employer's Council. This team of attorneys and educators conduct surveys throughout the Front Range of the Rockies, that include surveys of actual wages paid per type of job. Most companies have positions that have job descriptions and qualification requirements. These are easy to compare and establish fair market prices for types of services. Most large American corporations have similar positions throughout their businesses and they have rates that typically reflect the variances in the cost of living by geography. I owned a beautiful home on 15 glorious acres in Clifton, Texas, this cost me about $250,000. This same house would have cost over a million dollars in Fort Collins. These differences are significant. There was the same kind of information regarding pay rates for the Waco area, and of course, Dallas, Houston and any other American city. I believe in the free market, so I think these numbers are a wonderful starting point.

Each business has roles that have to be effectively played out each day for the entity to thrive and grow. Any mature industrial engineer should be able to go into your business and in short order, establish a matrix of tasks that are part of these roles. Most businesses from our ranch, to Subway, to IBM, have detailed job descriptions with qualification requirements. Begin with what is already there. These job descriptions are not work instructions, which is also part of this compensation salad. The goal is to have every person who works in your business become capable of understanding and doing each task. This goal requires a simple yet significant training program. The other goal is to have no supervisors or managers, only trainers, leaders and customer service representatives. The middle class is disappearing, so should middle management!

I have never taken over a plant in my life that wasn't "managed" by men, yet directly beneath most of them was a woman who did the tasks, understood the minutia, and covered his butt. The difference in their pay could be over 100%. This wasn't a "glass ceiling". This was simply an internally created female prison whose inmates are people with high intelligence and low self esteem. In order to see any ceiling, one has to look up. I have never seen discrimination against anyone be based on age, race, or sex in the workplace. It has been my experience that most companies have bent over backwards to avoid accusations of discrimination. If a minority person or woman was even closely qualified for a position, it has been my direct experience that pressure

200

has been put on me to use that person over an equally qualified white male. However, the people who best move the rock should get the job regardless of age, race, sex or handicap.

These middle "managers" who have assistants, are the first place to start. The acid test to me was to ask them to actually do the tasks that their trusted sidekick does, if he cannot, he should go! I have never taken over a business that didn't have several useless middle managers that had very productive assistants, NEVER! Effective managers rarely need an assistant, executives do.

Every other person in the organization is a customer service representative (CSR). The tasks that each CSR does will differ, but every activity is designed to best serve the customer. Some will clean the toilets, some will run the machinery and some will take orders. Others will do accounts payable tasks or collections or work in estimating. Whatever the tasks, the end goal is to please your customers. Making everybody a CSR puts the business' primary objective of pleasing the customer first the way we each identify ourselves.

We used task matrices in the employee lunch room that were under lock and key and covered an entire wall. On the horizontal axis was listed every job classification in the business. On the vertical axis was listed every employee. This board was magnetized and we used a blue colored dot to designate an employee "in training" and a red dot to designate a job that the employee had mastered enough to be able to train another. We had pay scales by job classification, but once a year we reviewed that wall and as people successfully completed the skills and time requirements, their dots changed from blue to red and a raise was awarded. After five years we had machine operators who made $18-$20 an hour, but they could do design work, scheduling and other jobs that they were fully qualified to fill in for. This 200 person plant operated at world class levels with one official salaried supervisor. We never even had any graffiti on our bathroom walls because our people went through a very extensive hiring process and they liked working there. We had extremely low turnover and we celebrated our accomplishments all of the time. We didn't hire people without the input of the team and a period of pre-employment, through a temp agency, that could last half a year or more. We did invest in engineering, training and human resource personnel, but not equal to the number of supervisors that would be in a typical plant of that size. We also were the quality leader in our industry and we were extremely profitable and had no lost time accidents or union.

We were acquired in 1995 and I stayed on as General Manager. The business unit was selected "Plant of the Year" twice. We were Kodak's premier supplier of packaging for years; we supplied Motorola and Hewlett Packard. I managed that small operation from 1996 until 2004 and we made over $20,000,000 in profit on about $210 million in sales during that time. I was promoted in 2005 and sent to our largest most troubled plant that was a $75 million dollar a year operation that was plagued with employee problems and running just a little better than break even. In 18 months, when I left to take over the ethanol project, we were turning a $1,000,000 a month profit, had completed one million man hours without a loss time accident and we were selected the plant with the Most Improved Work Environment in 2005 and the Most Improved Plant in 2006.

We could have done better, we actually had several salaried people that made over $100 grand a year that drank, hunted and played golf, but did little else but kiss my boss' butt. We could have easily fired them without skipping a beat and put another million dollars on the bottom line.

The skill based pay system rewards for flexibility and development of work habits that emphasize learning, performance and earning. We paid a premium to our people for premium work done. We charged a premium for our commodity product because we delivered premium results. Each individual in the organization had a quarterly performance matrix. This was meant to facilitate a quarterly dialogue between the leader and his followers that was integrated and informational. Each person had a set of seven basic objectives or goals. I picked seven because it is a special number. These matrices were needed to manage the skills board properly and to ensure that all positions were covered for cross training. The boards and matrices needed to be managed by tasks. The matrices were used to lead by aiding in communication and clarification of objectives. When people left their reviews, they knew what was expected of them for the next three months. When they cashed their quarterly bonus checks of $600 or more, they understood that profits yield increase and individual performance matters in how much of that profit one receives as a bonus. Profit and performance are the only reasons for earning extra money.

The first objective is safety. This is numerically measurable and each person will know where they stand with their bonuses as the safety numbers are posted. Every employee loses the entire bonus amount awarded for safety if there is a loss time accident during that quarter. Individual tasks or projects that are safety related will be briefly documented and these will be the objectives for the safety component of the bonus payout. If there are no accidents and one completes their projects or objectives, then they receive a score of 100% for the safety column on the matrix.

The second objective is productivity. This obviously is different for each job. All productivity is expressed as dollars of labor, or hours of labor required for a specified unit of output. All other efficiency numbers are nice for prompting corrective actions, but true productivity numbers and behaviors should be emphasized. Use good numbers that truly reflect improvements in output per hour. This is where we begin the "you are a slug" conversation. Keeping these objectives as numerical as possible and readily available, like the safety numbers, enables everybody to know where they stand in relation to their bonus payout. If they improve their work habits, meet their numerical objectives and play well with others, they will receive a 100% for the productivity column on the matrix. If they run at 130% or 70%, their score will be adjusted accordingly.

The third objective is quality. Like productivity, this varies from business type to business type, but within each industry the measurements for quality are usually consistently applied. Use the numbers that your business/market uses. Post these numbers regularly and collectively set objective goals for each quarter and document the tasks that each person will do to ensure they contribute to a leading quality position. If objectives are met and projects completed, then they receive a 100% on the quality column on the matrix.

The fourth objective is attendance. This is very simple and straightforward. If they miss time, they lose percentage points for the attendance column on the matrix. Each business will have to establish what works for them. A 100% is only given for perfect attendance.

The fifth objective is continuous improvement project implementation. Each person must be on a team for the conducting of a productivity study and have the solution IMPLEMENTED during the quarter in order to earn 100% for this column. You either get 100% or nothing. This used to have our maintenance department running like mad during the last three weeks of a quarter. Everybody needed their projects IMPLEMENTED, to get the payout percentage that goes on the continuous improvement column of the matrix. This is very important. Remember I stated that management guru

Peter Drucker said that the basic tasks of the managing is innovation and marketing. This set of objectives ensures that a, steady stream of innovative projects are always underway. This is where we chip away at eliminating or improving tasks that are not pleasant to do. This is where we learn to make things that our competitors cannot or will not. These objectives may include things like anger management or smoking cessation or weight loss. Again, sloth, gossiping and foolishness issues get documented here.

The sixth objective is training. This included an elaborate coordination on everybody's cross-training objectives to insure all positions, and people, received the appropriate hours of cross-training. The job descriptions should have a designated number of years required to be qualified to do the job and the tasks that need to be mastered. All offsite education and training programs and requirements for HAZMAT, or quality training etc. are included here. Due to the reluctance of leaders who have productivity objectives to always allow people to cross-train; these leaders can only receive a 100% on their own training component on their matrix, if all of their people complete their training objectives.

The last objective is marketability. This refers to the environment that our business exists in. Operation appearance, customer treatment and sales support go into the objectives on this column on the matrix. This must be tailored on a business by business basis. If you are a machine operator, this would include your workplace cleanliness and how well you present yourself to visiting customers or corporate folks. I always required a 24 hour turn around on quotes and samples. The industry norm was 5-10 days. This is where we differentiate ourselves as a team of Happy Americans, safely making good stuff, fast!

Once each objective receives a score they are simply added up and that is the individual quarterly performance score. This number is a percentage and is multiplied times the per hour profit allocation to establish each person's quarterly bonus payout. In my experience with the business I managed that did about $20,000,000 annually in sales, and had a 14% profit, with just under 200 employees paid out about $500 a quarter, to each person. This varied by each employee's wage level and hours worked per quarter. Some people received $300, while others may get $700.

Each year our labor costs as a percentage of sales remained unchanged. However, our people earned far above average for their pay, and earned more and more each year. This actually didn't affect the bottom line because we needed less people each year to produce more sales. I also got rid of my overpaid middle managers and replaced them with their female subordinates. At corporate my management team was referred to as my harem. But we performed as a world class organization for that period of time. We were the flagship plant for quality graphic packaging for a decade.

As we had to assimilate into the new corporate policies and practices, our skill based pay system was eliminated and they went out and hired supervisors. This plant which was built in 1986, run as a corporate division from 1995 until 2010; is permanently shut today. They lost their fleet-footedness, they became corporate with people to manage, and systems to be enslaved by, and now they're gone. I'm writing references today for their former employees.

So there you go managers. I have always told my people that I don't mind them calling me "all wet" as long as they said it while handing me a towel. That means; criticize all you want, but bring me a better plan while you do it. So if you want to bring negativity into any meeting, "don't forget to take a towel".

This is called the Integrated Management System. This system worked beautifully for over 8 years and the business ran wonderfully, safely and profitably. People had good countenances, we celebrated with food, parties and events all of the time when we collectively achieved milestones. Managers rarely left the business unless they were promoted. We were considered a training ground for managers and leaders. It was because we were all good followers! I thank God every day for that experience. I thank the many teachers I've had, especially Ed Parker, Deepak Chopra, Glenn Beck, Joel Osteen, Joyce Meyer and Stephen Covey.

This system, like all of them, need to be lived and improved upon year after year. There is no such thing as status quo. There are as many variations to this theme as there are different businesses. But the key components are: 1) Profitably running, 2) Good job descriptions, work instructions and standards, 3) Seven clear integrated objectives reinforced and discussed four times a year and a bonus awarded at that time for the previous quarter's performance, 4) Enough time and energy in training, engineering, and continuous improvement project IMPLEMENTATION, 5) make sure everybody takes time to move the rock, in fact, all tasks that don't directly move the rock should be challenged, and 6) CELEBRATE and honor followership and success.

Chapter 8

Onward

"Covetousness, anger and foolishness are things to sort out well. When bad things happen in the world, if you look at them comparatively, they are not unrelated to these three things. Looking comparatively at the good things, you will see that they are not excluded from wisdom, humanity and bravery."
(Yamamoto Tsunetomo, 1716)

Yamamoto Tsunetomo was a Samurai turned sage after his Lord Nabeshima Mitsushige died in 1700. He was forbidden from taking his own life, as was Samurai custom, so he retired to become a Buddhist priest. He wrote "Hagakure" a word that is translated as "hidden by the leaves". Yamamoto saw the dangers in coveting, cowardice and foolishness, as did Solomon, Moses, Chuang Tzu, Jesus, Buddha, Muhammad and others. It has never been more obvious than it is today.

We need to visualize a new world order that is not violent, feeds it's children of all ages, frees all of its people, honors mother earth and allows everybody to spend their time working to express their God-given gifts to reach their God-allowed destiny. I say God-allowed, not God-controlled. He gives us opportunity;

we need to do the work. We create ourselves every day. We control how healthy we are, how wealthy we are, how heavy we are and how smart we are. We choose to open the door when God has opportunity knock, or take a nap and sleep through it. We choose to spend our money on lottery tickets instead of putting it into the collection plate. We choose to watch another re-run of "CSI" or we can take a class on line. We choose to stop at the bar for a few, or stop and mentor a child. We choose to stop working when we lose our job, or we really step up the pace. We all have things that have taken a back seat to work for years, put them in the front seat, or maybe the driver's seat.

I suggest to all of you, to do a brutally honest personal inventory, with a critical eye towards coveting, sloth and gossiping. During this inventory be just as honest about your strengths and passions. Lastly, make a list of your teachers, bosses and brands and access how you could be a better student and follower. The changes in our world will continue to challenge our extravagant quality of life in America compared to the countries that we buy products from. As a result, the loss of our manufacturing base and associated jobs will continue. Job satisfaction will become more valuable than money, as it should be. Excellence in what we do and happiness in why we work will help us constantly improve how we work and how we protect one another and our environment. We should look deep inside before we buy a product made with slave labor, in atrocious working conditions, while polluting our world.

Joel Osteen is always inspirational and up-lifting. He always tells us that we are Holy, anointed, children of the Most High God. His message has been steadfastly optimistic regarding our ability to rebound from our economic woes, health problems, family issues and work challenges. He is non-denominational, which is essential in this day and age as far as I am concerned. It is time for Christians to leave it at that, not Catholic, Baptist, Methodist, yada, yada, yada. We believe that Jesus was the Messiah, the teller of truth, son of Mary and God, judge of mankind. We who seek God are all on different levels of the universal, spiritual, learning curve. Learning involves making mistakes. We demonstrate that we are learning from them by not making the same mistakes in the future. Unfortunately, many of these mistakes hurt others. It is the job of a Christian not to judge and to forgive. If people truly repent, and others truly forgive; things work out great. If we look at life as followers of a loving, forgiving God and try to emulate that, we will follow well and our bosses will happily afford us the opportunity to express ourselves when the time is right. God will do His job; just make sure to do yours.

I love being an American and everything that it stands for. We are at a time of man that is truly Biblical in proportion and what we individually and collectively do is critical to our health, prosperity, world peace and environmental balance. As we begin 2013 we need to ignite our passion for excellence and our love for being American. One Nation under God is who we are.

We need to begin with the Ten Commandments. We need to admit to chronically not following the covet code, the Sabbath rule along with the rules against foolishness, sloth and gossiping. Before we try anything new, let's try to do the old things correctly and see what that brings. As I said, I've not invented anything. I am being a typical consultant and borrowing your watch to tell you what time it is. It is time to get to work. There is much to do.

Our President is going to try to control his destiny, not ours. His goal is to be Ruler of the world. Man of the Year!? China is using North Korea like Tony Soprano directs his lieutenant to use an out of control meth-head to commit the most heinous crimes. North Korea will do the deed with Chinese made weaponry, satellites and strategies. Then China will sit back with their airtight alibi; "I was having dinner at Vesuvio's with the American President."

Do not let this man take away our rights to bear arms. Once we begin to dismantle our Bill of Rights, we begin to become something else. The shootings in schools, churches and shopping centers are tragic. When I heard of the shootings this week in Connecticut, I cried like many people around the world did. This is pure evil. It really scares me how passionate our President is as he sets the stage to disarm the American Patriot and divert attention from the economic tsunami approaching. He is using this tragedy to further his own agenda. The problem isn't guns anymore than automobiles are responsible for highway deaths.

If we focused our efforts to not allowing products to be sold in America that are made by slaves while polluting the environment, instead of gun control, then investment in America would quickly become more attractive and better jobs would be created. When mom and dad have good jobs that pay well and they don't over extend themselves, they will have more free time to love their children the way they wish they could every day.

Pay hardworking Americans enough to enable them to live their lives, not simply work them away. Stop paying people too much for doing too little and tax excessive income, excessively. There is no logic in stopping our income tax rates at 33% when income for the wealthiest continues to escalate at an obscene pace compared to the rest of Americans.

To the American Heroes, the people who work their butts off to make ends meet, the people who "Move the Rock"; military personnel, policemen, teachers, firefighters, mechanics, assemblers, burger flippers, truck drivers, cesspool cleaners, farmers, cowgirls, website designers, software creators, nurses, volunteers, people who live in their cars while they follow their dreams; THANK YOU and GOD BLESS YOU! We were created to work six days a week. Our brethren around the globe live in poverty. They would love a steady supply of food, clean water, shoes on their feet and a private place to poop. So in spite of how tough it is to work two jobs just in order to barely make ends meet, keep things in a global perspective if you intend to remain a global shopper. Don't compare yourself to the

Jones' down the street, compare yourself to people around the globe who do the same thing that you do for a living. See where you stand. Do you have anything to covet? Remember, we become wealthy when we cease from coveting. Stop buying things that we don't need, don't go into debt and be thankful. Our individual actions and countenance will determine our ability to heal and prosper. Our efforts day in and day out is what keeps America, "America".

To learn more about leading, following or American
Hero Response Training and personalized martial arts
contact: bobsmallwoodahrt@gmail.com

www.ingramcontent.com/pod-product-compliance
Lightning Source LLC
Chambersburg PA
CBHW071419170526
45165CB00001B/329